DONKEY
TALES

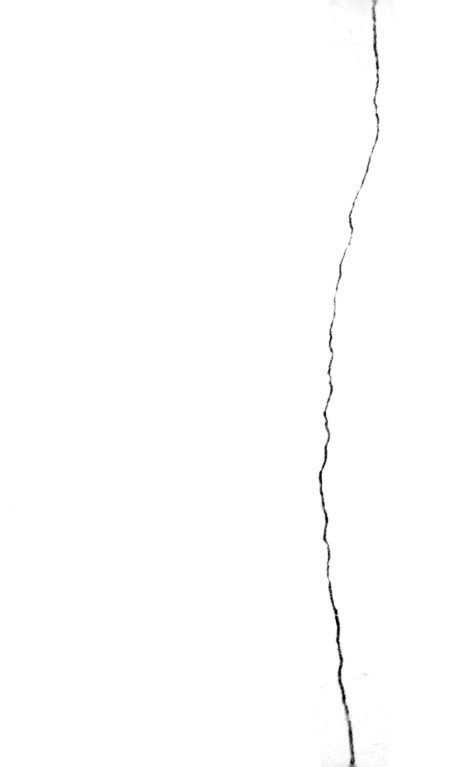

DONKEY TALES

Exploring Perspectives of the Bible's Stubborn Creatures

By

Keith Alexis

Bless you.
I Admire your
ministry.

WordCrafts

Published by WordCrafts Press
Tullahoma, TN 37388
www.wordcrafts.net

Contents

Dedication

Upon the completion of writing this book I could not wait to give the first copy of my raw first-draft to my dad. Throughout the process he always asked me about it and was anxious to see it. He made it a point to be his kids' biggest fan no matter what it was we were doing or working toward accomplishing. When I placed that copy in his hand, I did not know just a couple of months later on September 19, 2013, he would meet God face to face and start living his new life in eternity.

Daniel Benjamin "Bud" Alexis was without a doubt the greatest influence in my life. He was a faithful husband, a loving and supportive father, proud grandfather and a life-long minister of the Gospel. He will be deeply missed by family, friends and the many whose lives he touched. I dedicate this book to my Dad's memory because the things I have learned and shared in this book are built upon the foundation he established in my life.

Introduction

I was asked to play bass guitar in a band assembled to lead worship for a young-adult retreat. A young man by the name of Jason Smith spoke at the retreat. Jason had grown up in El Dorado, Arkansas, the same town where I lived and we both attended the same church. God called Jason into full-time Christian ministry and at the time of the retreat he was serving as a youth pastor at a church in Auburn, Alabama.

On the first night of the retreat Jason used the example of the donkey Jesus rode into Jerusalem to illustrate some of the points in his message. Listening to Jason speak about the relevance of the donkey, I began thinking about all the references throughout the Bible where donkeys were present during a significant event. "There just might be some important lessons we could all learn by looking at these stories through the eyes of the donkey," I thought.

If you are a preacher or teacher you will know what I mean when I say, some points when you hear them will cause you to spin off on a maze of ideas and applications for a newly planted thought. There I was sitting in the back of the room while Jason was speaking and my mind was racing through the Bible. I wondered, "How many other donkeys in the Bible have we overlooked that just might be there to teach us some sort of deep lesson?"

On the night's drive home from the retreat I had a strong sense this idea would make a great series for the adult Sunday school class I was teaching at the time. While it might be a little out of the box to announce, *we're going to study donkeys in the Bible*, everyone who knows me knows I'm no stranger to coloring outside the lines. If it is in God's Word, then I believe it is there for a greater reason and we need to study in such a way to allow the Holy Spirit to speak truth into the depths of our hearts.

It is easy to fall into the rut of studying the same stories and scriptures just because they are familiar. With this in mind, the opportunity to study obscure references in the Bible and learn something from them seemed like an adventure I couldn't resist taking.

The first challenge I had to overcome was the fact I did not know anything about donkeys. The only donkey I had ever had any experience with was a three-foot-high, concrete donkey that used to stand in my grandparents' rock garden in De Leon, Texas. As a small child I rode atop the donkey, holding on tightly to its ears for all I was worth. Years later, when my daughter and son were small children, I took great pleasure in taking them to my grandparents' house to ride that same donkey. I am happy to say; today the beloved lawn ornament sits in my parents' yard waiting for another generation of riders to come along.

Have you ever noticed the many ways donkeys appear in popular culture? The most famous is, of course, Donkey from "Shrek." One of my favorites is Eeyore from "Winnie the Pooh," who was named from the sound donkeys make. If you watch retro cartoons you may recognize this one as well, Baba Looey, Quick Draw McGraw's donkey sidekick. If you remember

"Grizzly Adams," Number 7 was Mad Jack's donkey. The long running variety show "Hee Haw" had a donkey mascot and in the old folk tale, "Town Musicians of Bremen," there was a donkey as the main character. In children's party games, there is only one animal to pin a tail on. As you can clearly see, there is no shortage of love for the donkey.

The very next morning my quest to research donkeys began. First, I found there were plenty of donkeys in the Bible for possible candidates. Since I had never before even touched a donkey, I thought it might be useful going forward to learn as much as I could about donkeys, especially if I planned to teach about them. I found donkeys were amazing creatures and there was a lot we could all learn from them.

Donkeys vary in height from around three to five feet at the withers, the highest point of the back which is usually at the base of the neck. The average life span of a donkey is thirty to forty years, with some living to over fifty years of age. A donkey is comparatively much stronger than a horse pound for pound. Their two main means of defense is their famous kick and a ferocious bite. Their loud bray can be heard for up to two miles away. Donkeys have a reputation for being stubborn animals, but the fact is they are intelligent, independent thinkers with a heightened sense of preservation.

Donkeys actually make decisions based on safety. Rather than just blindly obeying its master, the donkey will think about whether something is a good idea before it does it. A good donkey owner can train his donkey to obey him by gaining the trust of the animal. Once a donkey is convinced you will never do anything to hurt it, you are more likely to gain cooperation from your donkey.

It is my hope as you read through each chapter the scriptures will come alive in a new and fresh way. I know donkeys can't talk and therefore, some of what is written in the following pages are lessons revealed to me by the Holy Spirit as I studied the passages from a different perspective. It is my prayer God will use the tales from the mouth of a donkey to speak to your heart and bring encouragement to your spirit.

The time has come to place your blanket on the burro, jump on top and ride into the pages of a life-changing journey. Thanks for joining me; it's going to be one exciting ride.

Prologue
"Let there be...Donkeys?"

Actually, God never said, "Let there be donkeys." However, on the sixth day of the creation story found in the first chapter of Genesis God did say, "Let the earth bring forth the living creature according to its kind: cattle and creeping thing and beast of the earth, *each* according to its kind; and it was so."[1] Donkeys definitely fall into this category and did serve a special purpose during Biblical days as you will see in the following chapters.

Several Sundays passed before I announced the next series of lessons I planned to teach were about donkeys in the Bible. As you can probably guess, a few of my witty friends (a.k.a. "wise guys") asked, "Are you going to use the original word for *donkey* in the lessons?" I knew what they were talking about, but I thought it would be more fun to really use the original word for *donkey* found in the Hebrew text. If they want to say, *original,* then we can't quote from the King James Version, now can we?

There are actually two Hebrew words for donkey: Chămôr, which refers to a he-donkey and *'âthôn* which refers to a she-donkey. Today, the difference is marked affectionately as a jack for male donkeys, and a jenny for female donkeys.

The first domestication of donkeys was recorded in about 3,000 B.C. in or around Egypt. This proves man and donkey have a long-standing history together. Their use spread to the Middle East in about 1,800 B.C. Donkeys were in no way considered low class, rather they were a preferred method of travel. Many wealthy people rode on donkeys. Several people mentioned in the Bible as riding on donkeys also owned horses. Wealth was often marked by how many donkeys one owned. Donkeys in Biblical times were extensively used in trade as pack animals.

There are over 140 references to donkeys in the Bible. It is common to study great men and women in God's Word and learn the truths hidden in their stories. In the same way, I believe if donkeys were important enough to appear a large number of times in the Bible, there must be something we can all learn from them.

Comparing human behavior with animals is quite common. You can be *busy as a bee*, or *sly as a fox*. If you are *a snake* you are deceptive, but if you are *an owl* you are wise. We have *puppy love* and *bear hugs* from *mother hens* who tell you to stop *monkeying around*. You can be *silly as a goose*, but should try to avoid being as *big as a whale*. When someone is as *hungry as a bear* they may *wolf down their food* or even *pig out*. Lawyers are called *vultures*. Other characteristics include: *quick as a rabbit, slow as a turtle, clumsy as a bull in a china closet, strong as an ox, happy as a lark, slow as a turtle*, and *quiet as a mouse*. This said, for some reason most people do not take it complimentary when called a donkey.

Take a moment to read Genesis chapter 49. Jacob was giving a final word to all his sons. He says to his son, Issachar, He is a "strong donkey, lying down between two burdens."[2] Now if my dad said, "Keith, you're a strong donkey lying down between two burdens," my first thought would be, "Huh?" Then I would try to get to the bottom of exactly what such an odd statement meant so I could decide whether to be upset or not.

Did this scripture mean Issachar was lazy and would lie down instead of work? Donkeys are known to sit or lie down if their burden is too heavy. Let's look at Issachar's story to get a clearer idea of what kind of person he was.

Issachar, the Strong Donkey

It all started when Jacob met Rachel. He loved her very much and arranged to marry her. The story goes, when Jacob asked Rachel's Dad, Laban, for her hand in marriage, Laban made Jacob promise to work on his land for seven years in order to gain his blessing. Then, Laban would give his permission for Jacob to marry Rachel. However, before this wedding could come about, Jacob was tricked into first marrying Leah, Rachel's older sister. Jacob had to work for Laban an additional seven years for Rachel.

Leah had four sons by Jacob with the hope that bearing a quartet of strapping boys would make him love her. Still, Jacob loved Rachel. Eventually four more sons were born to Jacob by the maids of both Rachel and Leah; apparently there was a competition going on.

One day Rueben, Leah's oldest son, came in from the field with some mandrakes and he gave them to his mother. When Rachel sees the mandrakes she asks Leah if she can have some of them. Leah responds, "You already have my husband, and now you want my mandrakes, too?" From this we can assume Jacob had very little to do with Leah.

Rachel comes up with a clever deal for Leah. If Leah will give Rachel the mandrakes, in exchange, Rachel will give Jacob to Leah for the night. When Jacob came home from the field that evening, Leah informed him of the deal she had made with Rachel. Jacob was Leah's for the night.

"Now what is the big deal about mandrakes?" you may ask. A mandrake is a small yellow fruit planted in the ground and grown like a potato. It was believed to have medicinal and magical powers. The literal Hebrew interpretation for the word "mandrake" was "love plant" and believed to ensure fertility. Ah ha! Rachel, still barren, was desperate to have those mandrakes in hopes they would help her become more fertile and better able to give Jacob a son, the one thing to this point, she had been unable to do. By the looks of things the mandrakes were apparently working well for Leah.

Issachar was conceived on the night Jacob was exchanged for the mandrakes and Leah declared, "God has given me my wages." The name Issachar means "he will bring reward," and from the day he was born moving forward he carried with him the stigma of being for hire.[3]

Moses declared a joint prophesy to Zebulun and Issachar in his final blessing given to the tribes of Israel. "Rejoice, Zebulun, in your going out and Issachar in your tents."[4] After settling in Canaan, where the land of these two tribes abutted one another, Zebulun became a trader of commerce and Issachar became a keeper of the Torah studying the principles of the law.

Issachar had famous study tents in which they spent hours together studying the law. It seemed

Issachar had found rest and satisfaction in the place they had carved for themselves. Even though they were often seen as lazy and choosing to take the easy way out, Issachar showed unusual insight and strength.

The tribe of Issachar was one of the first tribes to side with David over Saul. They were sensitive to the fact God had anointed another. When the kingdom was divided, they were in the Northern Kingdom, yet its members attended Hezekiah of Judah's Passover feast.[5] They were true worshippers and seekers of God despite their circumstances and status. Just like Issachar had a heart to seek God, God calls each one of us to be a "strong donkey" eager to study His Word and be true worshippers who pursue Him.

The intent of this study is not just to learn about some donkeys in the Bible. It is to learn about the stories and situations surrounding the mention of the donkey. Some of these stories you will recognize, yet others you may have never known were even in the Bible. I hope you will have fun on this journey as you gain new insights into God's Word and find fresh truths to help you walk a little closer to your Savior.

Chapter 1
The Donkey Who Carried Jesus

In 1982 I attended my first Christian rock concert. Petra was performing in Shreveport, Louisiana, on their "More Power to Ya" tour. The lights dimmed and the thickest smoke I had ever seen to date filled the arena. The stage lights danced and the thunderous music powered forth like a mighty army storming a castle. The bass rattled my insides. As the fog started to disperse, I could faintly see figures dressed in camouflage-themed outfits appear on the stage. Gripping their respective instruments with authority, the band began to play and the crowd went wild. "Now THAT'S a triumphal entrance!"

For nine years I toured as a part of the Christian band *Tinman Jones.* We too had a flare for the dramatic as our goal was for visual appeal to accompany our music. At the onset of each show an intro track would start to play, laying a high energy foundation to build anticipation. At one point we had samples from our namesake, "The Wizard of Oz," layered in the track. As we took our places and donned our respective instruments, the Tin Woodsman would say, "Oh! It ticks..." This was the cue for the drummer to click his sticks together to give the rest of us the cadence for the first song.

There are many ways to make an entrance on a grandiose scale. Our sports heroes often ride through the streets amidst a rain of ticker tape and fanfare. I've seen people parachute into stadiums dressed like Elvis. Often, a flowery introduction is made by a prominent figure.

What did Jesus do? He rode in on a donkey! Here, at the greatest single act on the stage of mankind, we find Jesus making His grand entrance atop a little, short, stubby and smelly donkey. From a mere human perspective, one might think Jesus could have really benefited from a better P.R. (Public Relations) Person.

The prophet Zechariah, years before, had declared the messiah's method of transport. We read his words in Zechariah 9:9, "Behold, your King is coming to you; He *is* just and having salvation, Lowly and riding on a donkey, A colt, the foal of a donkey." Jesus was obligated to fulfill all prophesy so the donkey was a required participant in the story.

To set the stage, take a little time and read Matthew 21:1–9, Mark 11:1–10 and Luke 19:28–38. We see in these verses, Jesus was about to come to Jerusalem. On the journey they stopped at a place called Bethphage, close to the Mount of Olives, where Jesus sent two of His disciples to a village opposite them. He told them, once they arrived at the village they would immediately see a donkey tied up. They were to loose the donkey and bring it to him, because this was the donkey he would ride into Jerusalem.

Jesus' entrance into Jerusalem was an important day leading one to ask the question, why a donkey?

There is definitely some good scrub (donkey food) in this story to be harvested.

The Donkey Was Young

In all three accounts of Matthew, Mark and Luke, the donkey is referred to as a colt. In Matthew's version, it seems the donkey's mother was even present. Just how young was this donkey Jesus sent for? Well, a donkey's joints and bones are not mature enough for work until it is about three years old. It will reach full size at about four or five, and does not mature behaviorally until around six years old. For estimation purposes let's say the donkey was at least four years old.

Do you agree that *young* is a relative term? When you are a child, there are many things that you are too young to do. Amusement parks display signs marking the height one must be in order to get on the ride. You must prove you are *big enough*. Do you remember sitting at the kids' table and wishing you were old enough to sit with the big people at special dinners? Teenagers often think they are old enough to do just about anything, yet they can still be too young to drive, too young to vote or too young to be hired for certain jobs. I remember well when my son, Jamin, was applying for a summer job between college semesters. Over and over he would hear, "You must be 21 get the job." He felt this qualification was unfair as he believed he was plenty qualified at a younger age to perform the available positions well.

Dan Quayle was ridiculed relentlessly for being too young to hold the office of Vice President. Does anyone remember the endless late night spoofs of Quayle in the knickers and beanie cap? Yet, he was 41 years old with a long string of qualifications. There will always be things we desire to do for which we are considered too young. For most of us, 65 years old will be too young to retire.

Besides not meeting age requirements, there are other situations in life for which we may be considered too young. Have you ever moved to a new town where everything feels new and foreign? You don't know anyone, and fitting in seems to be a struggle. Maybe you started attending a new church and everyone already had their friendships established. Or it could be the things you participated in at your previous church don't exist in your new family of worship.

Growing up, my family moved around many times. As a matter of fact we were homeless for three years during my childhood. We were not destitute but we did not have a place to call home - basically, because we didn't need one. My dad was a preacher, and for those three years he was a traveling evangelist. In those days revivals took place from Sunday morning through Friday night. Each week for fifty weeks out of the year my family lived in a different town. Saturdays were devoted to traveling from one destination to the next. With my Dad preaching on the evangelistic field, as well as assuming several pastorate roles, I became really good at being the "new guy." I can honestly say I would not trade these years for anything, even though they did give me a fair share of challenges.

Whether you are too young to enjoy certain things in life or you don't have the qualifications to meet certain opportunities, the truth is, every one faces challenges in life. People new to a faith in Christ also qualify as being young. When Paul said, "Behold, all things have become new..."[6] he wasn't kidding. There is a reason why "new" Believers are also referred to as "baby Christians." With one decision comes many changes, not bad changes but changes all the same. All of a sudden, one moves from looking at life from a human perspective to viewing life from a heavenly perspective. Some things just look and feel different. It seems there is so much to learn including a new language full of terms that may sound strange compared to a strictly secular vocabulary.

Have you ever felt like you were too young or too lacking in maturity to be useful to God? If we are honest, we have all experienced times when we felt inadequate, lacking in knowledge, awkward or inferior when comparing ourselves to everyone else. We shy away from getting involved because we feel someone else may be more qualified. It's easy to think God might rather use *older* people to fulfill His purposes. And all the while we feel stuck sitting at the kids' table longing for a chance to hang out with the grown-ups.

Perhaps you are young in years or young in faith. You may be new to a church or new to a city. Whatever way you may face the challenge of being young, I am certain you relate to our donkey in this story.

Tied Up

Jesus told two of his disciples the donkey they were looking for would be tied. Being *tied up* is a phrase most of us can relate to. A common response when you ask someone to do something for you or with you is often, "I can't...I'm tied up right now."

We are often strapped to the hitching post by so many things in our lives. You may feel tied to a demanding job that totally consumes your time and leaves you feeling stuck with little opportunity of escape. Maybe you feel bound by some sticky circumstance and can't seem to find a way out. Debt is another obstacle holding many in bondage as every day more people are finding themselves in over their heads and drowning in a sea of never ending financial obligations. Sometimes we feel as if we are suffocating under our many daily commitments, feeling totally overwhelmed and unable to breathe.

The disciples find the donkey tied up to a post along a road at the entrance to a city and unable to move very far. We've all experienced times like this in our own lives haven't we? I know I've had times in my life when I can totally relate to the spot the donkey is in.

How does the view look when you are tied up? *The view always looks the same, doesn't it?* Whatever you are seeing is all you are ever going to see as long as you are fixed to the same spot. The routine of our daily lives can resemble being tied up. We wake up at the same time every morning and go through the same routine. Flip through the same channels and see the same television programs. We leave for work at the same time every day, take the same path and see the same people at the same red light. Once we get to work we have the same conversations. Occasionally, we may stop and wonder, "Is there anything else?" This donkey may have felt the same way as he stood there tied to this post.

It is possible to simply appear as if you are tied. Have you ever watched a good, old western movie? It always interests me to see the cowboy ride up to the hitching post, dismount his steed and throw the reigns over the post, not even tying it, just laying the straps over the post. Yet the horse does not run away. Why? Because the horse *thinks* it is tied up. However, given the right circumstances, if spooked or the horse senses the presence of impending danger, the pseudo-tied horse will bolt and run away. As long as it thinks it is tied up, the horse will continue to stand unmoved and in place.

I have a younger sister named LaDonna. We have always gotten along great. One day I felt the need to torture her, as older brothers are obligated to do from time to time. I took her to her room and tied her to the bedpost using my best Royal Ranger knots. Royal Rangers were similar to Boy Scouts and existed within my church affiliation. I amassed a chest full of badges to prove I was no slacker at knot tying. After I finished securing LaDonna to the bedpost I put a song on her stereo from our parents' old time Southern Gospel collection. I cranked it up as loud as it would go and ran. You may love Southern Gospel singing, but as kids it was far from our favorite music to listen to. This may sound far-fetched, but I kid you not, before I could get back to the doorway of my room, LaDonna untied herself, caught up to me and preceded to give me a pounding.

To this day I do not know how she released herself from my expert bindings. The point is, with the right motivation you can break any chains tying you down or holding you in bondage. Whether real or perceived, too many people find themselves in a state of bondage, choosing to remain "tied down" just like the donkey. Often times we expend all of our energy waiting and hoping to someday be released, rather than using our energy as LaDonna did to find a way out and overcome our circumstances.

Never Been Ridden

Can't you just imagine the poor donkey standing there tied to a pole and unable to go anywhere? Every day the donkey watched a parade of other donkeys go by carrying riders, hauling merchandise and doing all sorts of the great things donkeys are born to do.

There are many areas where donkeys really do come in handy. The obvious is transportation. Donkeys were the number one means of transportation in those times and most families had at least one. We also know donkeys were used to carry goods to market. A lesser known use includes placement within herds of sheep and goats for protection. Donkeys are possessive creatures and will attack wolves and even lions with their dangerous kick and bite to keep the flock safe. Donkeys are still used to this day as stablemates for race horses. Horses are more high spirited and when a trainer needs to calm a horse down he can stable it with a donkey and the calm demeanor of the donkey will have a quieting effect on the horse.

Have you ever wanted to do something for the Lord so badly, but you didn't know what to do? You look around and see others teaching, singing, serving, operating cameras and helping with many other ministries, and you pray, "God, You seem to have something to do for everyone but nothing for me. Here I am tied to this post with nothing to do."

As a boy I was not blessed with much substance on my skeleton. I was a scrawny kid to say the least. Unfortunately, I seem to have currently over-compensated for my previous deficiencies, but that's a different story. On top of my wiry frame, I wasn't an incredibly gifted athlete either. I remember standing against the wall in the gym during Physical Education Class while the team captains picked their players. I always seemed to be the last one picked. "You can have Keith," one would say. To which the other replied, "I don't want him, you take him."

If they were to ask me, I really did have a preference. To mark differences in the teams we played "shirts and skins," meaning one team would play shirtless and the other would wear shirts. I was a modest kid and hated showing my rib cage to the world, so I would pray, "God, let the *shirt* guy be the unlucky one today." Do you find it interesting you rarely hear stories from the first ones who were picked? Somehow it just seems every one of us in the world were always the last ones picked.

The point is at some time or another most of us have experienced what it is like to be the last one standing while feeling unwanted and devalued. There stood the donkey, having never been ridden and branded unimportant. Maybe some of its donkey friends would come by and bray, "Look what I get to do." The donkey, reflecting on its own young life, may have wondered if it will ever get to do anything of importance. "Surely someone will come along and pick me for a job." We all want to feel like we serve a purpose. We want our existence to matter.

Standing in His Own Mess

Please allow me to embellish the story a little here. This point isn't recorded in scripture, but it's worth some attention because it is significant to the plight of our donkey. The owner of the donkey was said to be nearby. Therefore, we can assume someone was taking care of this donkey. The donkey had to be fed to survive, and if the donkey eats, he must also…well, you know. Just where do you think the donkey made his mess? You guessed it; right where he was standing. Not only was this young donkey tied up and unable to do much of anything; it was watching all the other donkeys around it fulfill a purpose while it was standing smack dab in the middle of its own mess.

Have you ever felt like you were standing in the middle of your own self-made mess? It is easy to feel like there is no way out because you are tied up. Life's mess piles up and gets deeper and deeper until you can't see any opening in sight for rescue or relief. Sometimes it feels as if all hope is gone.

I told you a story about my sister; now in fairness I will tell you a story about my younger brother, Bryan. Bryan is eight years younger than me and while growing up we were privileged to share a room. We laugh today about the houses we lived in and the sizes of the rooms we shared. It always seemed our sister got the largest of the bedrooms while we shared the smallest.

As a teenager, I liked my things organized, in order, straight and put away neatly. Bryan didn't share my affinity for order. One day I thought I would be smart and trap him into straightening up his toys. I piled everything covering the floor onto his bed thinking he would have to put away his stuff in order to get in his bed.

When I came home later that night, I eased into the room expecting to find everything put away according to plan. Instead, what I found was a little brother sleeping soundly in his bed blanketed by his toys. He didn't move a thing. He just crawled under the mess and slipped into his dreams.

It is true that we can be in the midst of our mess for so long that we become comfortable. Our difficulties may seem insurmountable but at least it is our chaos. Why do you suppose this is? Perhaps it's because we know what we are up against while living in our familiar mess and we often find ways to manage the damage while maintaining a thin string of sanity without having to change anything.

What the Donkey Didn't Know

One of the biggest mistakes we make when we feel young, tied up, useless and in the middle of a huge mess is thinking Jesus doesn't know where we are. We feel as if we are a missing flight on God's heavenly radar and there is no blip on the screen representing our plight. Believing you are so unnoticed by God could not be further from the truth. Jesus called two of His disciples and told them exactly where to find the donkey they were to retrieve. Nowhere does it say he had gone ahead to scout out where all available donkeys might be. He knew instantly where the donkey was located. You can lay your head on your pillow tonight and know Jesus knows where you are. He sees you. You are never lost from his view. God promises us, "'Am I a God near at hand,' says the Lord, 'And not a God afar off? Can anyone hide himself in secret places, so I shall not see him?' says the Lord;".[7]

I remember making my first "C" on my report card. I found fifth-grade science challenging. Realizing I was in great trouble and my life would soon be over, I took the only reasonable course of action. Slinking into the front door I put my report card on the TV, and penned a note saying something like this, "Dear Mom and Dad, I have made a 'C' on my report card and have decided to run away." After packing a few things I headed down the road. Finding a comfortable place in a ditch behind a culvert literally within full view of my house I made camp. My mom's version of the story reveals when they came home they could see my little cotton-top head poking above the culvert and knew I was okay. They patiently waited for my return knowing full well I would eventually get hungry and come home for supper. I thought I was deep in hiding and they would be worried about me. However, they knew exactly where I was the entire time.

Have you ever packed up a few things and headed down the road of life because you thought you had messed up too badly for God to ever use you? God looks down the road and sees you where you are, and watches over you until you are ready to come back home and into His arms. David said it best,

"O Lord, You have searched me and known me. You know my sitting down and my rising up; You understand my thought afar off. You comprehend my path and my lying down, and are acquainted with all my ways. For there is not a word on my tongue, But behold, O Lord, You know it altogether. You have hedged me behind and before, And laid Your hand upon me. Such Knowledge is too wonderful for me; It is high, I cannot attain it. Where can I go from Your Spirit? Or where can I flee from Your presence? If I ascend into heaven, You are there; If I make my bed in hell, behold, You are there. If I take the wings of the morning, and dwell in the uttermost parts of the sea, Even there Your hand shall lead me, And Your right hand shall hold me."[81]

Find comfort in knowing wherever you are and in the midst of whatever you may be dealing with today, God sees you. You are never lost from his sight.

Jesus Had Purpose for the Donkey

As Christians, the most common question many of us constantly wrestle with is, "What is God's will for my life; what is my purpose?" Although each of our lives may take different paths, the answer to this question is the same for every believer. It is the same purpose Jesus had for this donkey, to carry Christ into the world. In the book of Mark, Jesus says, "…'Go into all the world and preach the gospel to every creature.'"[8]

This colt of a donkey had an awesome opportunity and responsibility on this historic day, to carry Jesus into Jerusalem and into the final chapter of his life before the cross. We have equal opportunity and responsibility every day to carry our savior into our work place, our neighborhoods, our schools, our homes and even into the local grocery store.

We have a tendency to make things complicated in life when it comes to following the will of God. Too often when opportunities present themselves for us to carry Christ we respond, "Well, I better pray about it." I'm not trying to downplay the importance of prayer in our lives, however sometimes we use this statement as an excuse to opt out of what God is opening up for us to do. Prayer can become a stall tactic we use until we can come up with a better reason to say no. You do not have to pray about whether to witness to your coworker. There are no signs from above necessary when it comes to being a good neighbor or showing compassion to another. You have the green light from God for all the above at any time and in any place. Many times we want to hear the audible voice of God before carrying out a specific assignment. We want Him to show us the entire mission before we are willing to take the first step or make the first move. The mission is simple, as believers we are called to a specific purpose: To carry Christ into a lost world.

Rescue Is on the Way

The third thing the donkey didn't know is Jesus had staged a rescue for this young donkey to be set free. Jesus sent two of his disciples to untie the donkey and bring it to him. You must realize no matter what your situation is, regardless of how big the mess may be you have made for yourself, whether or not you are too young or too old, Jesus not only knows where you are and what he has planned for you, he has set things into motion for you to be freed so you can carry out His purpose.

One of my favorite chapters in the Bible is Romans chapter eight. One of my favorite verses reads, "And we know that all things work together for good to those who love God, to those who are the called according to His purpose."[9] It is important to know the verse does not mean you will be immune from bad situations in life. What is does mean is God will take the broken pieces of your life and put them back together to make something beautiful and good. We stand at a disadvantage because we can only see from one limited vantage point in our lives, but God sees from all angles and into the future. He orchestrates people and events all around you to facilitate your rescue long before a situation arises.

You may remember the story of Joseph, the favored son, who left home to find his older brothers. When they saw him approaching, they seized him, took his coat of many colors and threw him in a pit, intending to kill him. God arranged for a caravan of traders to wander at the perfect time giving an opportunity for the brothers to sell Joseph into slavery instead of having his blood on their hands.

The story goes on to reveal God was transporting Joseph to Egypt for the purpose of saving his family from famine. What I notice in this part of the story is God had to set the band of traders on a course to the pit long before Joseph even left his house earlier the same morning in order for them to be there at just the right time. The next time you feel like your situation is hopeless, or you think God has forgotten you, be reminded somewhere there is help on the way. God knows where you are tied up and has dispatched the rescue team to show up at exactly the right time.

It Wasn't All Smooth Sailing

It would have been great if the story ended with Jesus sending the rescuers to untie the donkey and they all lived happily ever after. However there is more to the story, as there often is after we experience a supernatural rescue. Our donkey had three major challenges to face after being untied. Do you remember a time when you embarked on a mission from God and were met with challenges you had to overcome? Our donkey had some challenges of his own to face and overcome.

Jesus knew ahead of time he would be met with immediate opposition. He prepared the disciples he had assigned the task of untying the donkey that if someone tried to question them they were to reply, "The Lord needs it." It was a good thing Jesus prepared them, for just as they were releasing the animal from the hitch, a man called out, "Hey! What do you think you are doing?" You can be certain, as soon as you step out to do what you feel God has called you to do, someone close to you will discourage you or may even try to stop you. They may tell you, "You can't do that! You aren't old enough (or are too old) to take on those responsibilities!" You may hear, "You do not have any experience in what you are about to do!" Maybe even, "Look at the mess you have made out of everything you have done before!" When you step out and follow Christ on a daring mission your faith reveals to others their lack of pursuing their own call in Christ.

Joseph received an exciting and promising dream from God. Maybe he should have shown a little restraint in his enthusiasm to tell everyone what the Lord had shown him, but he was just a young boy who spoke without considering the outcome. He found those he loved were not very supportive. His father rebuked him and his brothers plotted to kill him, all because his vision for his future was grand. I believe the pit Joseph's brothers threw him into and used to hold him until they sold him into slavery was the turning point in Joseph's life. From Joseph's vantage point below the surface of the ground there was only one way to look...up. Joseph kept his eyes on the Lord from the moment he entered the pit instead of trusting his fate to those around him.

Before my band moved into full-time touring we were weekend warriors, usually playing three concerts per weekend. We worked regular jobs during the week and met up after work on Fridays to travel an hour or two for the first night's gig. Our Saturday performance was often another 12-hour drive from that location. We tried to work in a Sunday night concert at a venue along our trip back. Sometimes we did not make it home until the early morning hours. This gave us only a short time to sleep before returning to work on Monday. We considered this worthwhile because it was what we knew God had purposed for us to do.

I remember when a friend of mine who was a bit older pulled me aside one day. He spoke to me out of an honest heart of sincerity as he expressed his concern. He explained how he had always held my faith in great esteem but was worried I was headed down a dangerous path with all this rock music and dyed hair. "I don't understand how this can be Christian," he said. I tried my best to explain about the opportunities we had to minister to young people in the places we played. Another man, a supervisor, had purchased our first CD just to be supportive. He returned the next day and announced, "I don't like your music at all!" Of course, there were no refunds.

Have you ever experienced great disappointment because friends or family did not understand or support you as you stepped out to follow God's direction in your life? It may hurt you when the ones you hoped would be your biggest supporters are actually the ones trying to dissuade your effort to step out and carry Christ. What can we learn from this story? Jesus is already aware of these negative voices and he is perfectly able to give you the strength to move past your toughest critics and voices of disappointment.

You Try Walking on This

Imagine the scene as Jesus rode into the city where the excited crowd took off their coats and laid them in the path and tossed palm leaves onto the street. Can't you feel their excitement and the pleasure they must have felt as they bestowed honor upon their coming savior? Now think about it for one moment from the donkey's point of view. Have you ever walked bare foot over palm leaves? They are stiff, have sharp edges, and would never make a comfortable floor covering. Of course, I speak as one who is a self-admitted tenderfoot. I've been accused of sleeping in my shoes, which is totally not true, although you won't see me skipping barefoot across glass or a hot bed of coals, gravel or even a plush grassy knoll.

Earlier I explained donkeys have a heightened sense of self-preservation which is often mistaken as stubbornness. Through the donkey's point of view it could look like people were randomly throwing obstacles in its way to try and trip it. The donkey could have easily just stopped in his hooves as if to say, "I'm not walking over this debris!"

When you begin working for the Lord in what you feel He has called you to do, you will encounter obstacles. There will be sticks and prickly objects thrown at you. You may encounter unexpected challenges making it difficult to walk this uncomfortable path. When you have to tiptoe across potential stumbling blocks it isn't the time to sit down and give up. Christ is with you to empower, enable and encourage you to keep moving forward. Just like our donkey, you can walk right over those obstacles choosing not to turn away, buck, bray or stop short of the goal ahead of you. These are the times you must determine in your heart, 'I will...until.'

Facing the Mob

The shouting and singing may have sounded like praise to human ears, but to the donkey it was nothing but an unruly, yelling mob. This donkey was from Bethphage, a quiet, off the beaten path town few even knew about. Jesus took this donkey from a quiet, small village straight to the big city where people were pushing, yelling and throwing things. This was quite a change of environment. Likewise, God has a way of leading us out of our comfort zones and into new environments. In Isaiah God tells us: "Behold, I will do a new thing, now it shall spring forth; shall you not know it? I will even make a road in the wilderness and rivers in the desert."[10]

Playing with the band Tinman Jones most of our concerts took place in churches, Christian venues, camps and youth events. One time we were asked to play for an event at Disney World. Playing in Mickey Land sounds awesome, except for the tiny detail of where we would be playing.

Our performance was staged on Paradise Island, which is known as the "happiest place on Earth" but for an entirely different reason. Here, we played for an older, less sober crowd, most of whom did not look like our normal audience members. The easiest thing would have been to say, *we don't play in places like this*, and skip on down to play a nice little concert for a church camp. Yet, we felt compelled to see what God would do through us at Disney World.

Throughout the course of the night we had many opportunities to talk with people about why we were *different*. I don't know if our witness and the conversations we had with the crowd ever turned into anything fruitful, but I know in my heart God taught me a lesson in finding value in continuing to walk where he leads even when it feels uncomfortable and different.

Donkeys are more useful in some situations than horses because of their notably calmer demeanor. They are less likely to get spooked and rattled in unsettling situations than their more high-spirited cousins. This is a useful trait we can share with the donkey as we follow Christ into the ever changing landscape of His path for our lives.

Whatever your calling is, don't hold back. Find release from the things that tie you down and hold you in bondage from carrying Christ into a broken world. Don't stay stuck in your own mess, rather seek freedom in Christ. He knows your name, He sees you, and He created you to do great things for Him. Let God break the ties that bind you and just as the donkey found, there is an incredible adventure ahead created just for you to enjoy.

Chapter 2
The Good Donkey

Let's take a look together, from a different perspective, at a story commonly referred to as The Good Samaritan. In Luke's Gospel, Jesus tells a parable of a Jewish man who, when traveling from Jerusalem to Jericho, is attacked by thieves. Two religious guys pass by the beaten man without offering help. Eventually, a hated Samaritan comes by and rescues the man. This Samaritan takes the helpless man to a bed and breakfast where he can recover from his injuries.[11]

Tucked away in this familiar story is the mention of the Samaritan's donkey. It was the donkey that transported the fallen victim to safety. If this heroic figure is able to eternally wear the crown "The Good Samaritan," then his donkey that did the heavy lifting should be called "The Good Donkey!" Before we dissect the donkey's role in the story, let's explore a little background from the scene in play.

Jericho is about 18 miles east-northeast of Jerusalem, and seven miles from the Jordan River. Jerusalem sits at an elevation of around 2,500 feet above sea level while Jericho sits about 800 feet below sea level, making the journey a descent of about 3,333 feet. When Jesus said in verse 30 of our text the man went "down to Jericho" he wasn't kidding.

The path from Jerusalem to Jericho was extremely treacherous. The journey snaked through a rocky maze and became very narrow in some places. It was about an eight-hour journey by foot for the average person.

In writings by Josephus, the famed first century historian, some 40,000 men who were employed to work on the temple were suddenly excused from their jobs causing a flood of unemployment. Many of these jobless workers became *highwaymen*, thieves who preyed on travelers. Their actions caused the road to be known as *The Way of Blood.*

The Characters

We do not know much about this man who fell victim to the thieves. We know he was Jewish, he was traveling alone and he must have had something of value or he would not have been a target for robbery. These highway thieves were out-of-work fellows who had turned to a life of crime out of desperation. They looked to assault a profitable traveler. The man must have put up a fight since the robbers beat the man and left him for dead.

The next two characters we see in this story are the priest and the Levite. You may have heard the sermons or listened to the Sunday school lessons about these two evil, selfish, uncaring souls who were too busy and self-righteous to stop and help someone in need. Has it ever occurred to you, in our quickness to judge the actions of the priest and Levite, we are being just as self-righteous and judgmental as they were to the helpless Jewish man? Now, look with me at another perspective on the priest and Levite.

First, let's consider the priest. An estimated 12,000 priests lived in Jericho and made the trip to Jerusalem to perform rituals and ceremonies. Priests had strict rules about what they could and could not do. They were forbidden to touch anything dead, as this would make them unclean and unable to make sacrifice to God. In the books of the law God gave the priests strict statutes they were to follow to the letter and if they went against them they faced serious consequences. If we put ourselves into the priest's shoes for a moment and consider what was required of him, we may not be so quick to rush to judgment.

Next, let's consider the Levite. He was a temple assistant charged with following similar rules as those of the priest. It was the Levite at least who walked closer to the injured man to glimpse a closer look. The man was so seriously wounded it was too difficult for the Levite to determine if he were dead or alive. The Levite, obviously thinking more about his own safety, turned away from the man and crossed over to the other side where he continued on his way. Keep in mind robbery was common on this road. Therefore, it probably wasn't the first time they had passed someone beaten and lying helpless.

We Are Not So Different

We live in a hectic, fast-paced society. We have places to go, times to arrive at those destinations and very little wiggle room in-between. If we are honest with ourselves, we are just as likely to pass by the obvious needs of others on our way to an appointment with no time to stop. Not only has time become a consideration in our modern society, there are crafty scams of which to be mindful as well. We have been desensitized to the needs around us often due to the overwhelming number of campaigns for one cause after another. We cannot possibly give to every cause so it becomes easier to check "none of the above" than to sift through the bombardment of pleas to determine what we are willing and able to support.

One night, my wife, Terri, and I were driving home from her parents' house at about one o'clock in the morning. The road was dark and the trip was about an hour and a half in length. At the time, we had two sleeping toddlers in the back seat. We were about 45 minutes into our journey when I rounded a curve and spotted a man lying halfway out in the opposite lane of the road. Hitting the brakes hard, I slowed to a stop a short distance beyond the mysterious gentleman. I yelled to Terri, "There's a dude laid out in the road!" I made sure all the doors were locked, drove a bit further in search of a place to turn around so I could take another pass at the scene.

Several scenarios raced through my head, one being, "If I stop to help, his buddies may jump out of the bushes and rob us, or hi-jack the car." With two precious young ones to protect, I couldn't take any chances. I slowly passed by and confirmed there was indeed a man lying in the road. As I turned the car around again I spied a farm house just about a quarter-mile off the road. I turned onto the side road and made my way up the driveway of an old white house. I thought the best thing for me to do was call the sheriff and let the proper authorities handle the situation. This was definitely the safest option where my family was concerned. I knocked loudly on the door but there was no answer.

I backed out of the drive and headed toward the highway when another car pulled slowly onto the road. I stopped as they approached. They motioned for me to roll down my window then asked what we were doing. I asked them if they had a phone nearby. They questioned my need for a phone. I exclaimed without thinking, "There's a dude in the road around the curve!" The response we received was not at all what we were expecting. "He's our dad! We've been looking for him," they replied anxiously. I offered a quick reply, "You might want to get him out of the road." The two backwoods gentlemen further instructed, "We will take care of it. No need to call the cops or anything."

To this day I have no idea what set of events led to the man lying in the road. I often wonder if was he dead or passed out drunk? Although the question still haunts me, it does give some insight into passing by on the other side. While we are all called to help one another when we see a need, at the same time, it is important to use discernment as to the best and safest manner with which to offer assistance.

Why A Samaritan?

I have always found it interesting how Jesus chose to tell a heroic story using a Samaritan as the main character. The Samaritans and the Jews each hated the other. Samaritans preferred being referenced as Israelites because they claimed they were actual descendants of Ephraim and Manasseh who, when the rest of the Jews where carried away into Babylonian exile, remained behind keeping true to the ways of God and continuing to worship God in accordance to law. The Samaritans believed the Jews brought with them tainted beliefs from pagan religions when they returned from captivity.

The Jews believed the real descendants of Ephraim and Manasseh had been carried away by Assyria. They thought the King of Assyria had replaced them with people from other lands and brain-washed these relocated immigrants into thinking they were of Israel. The Jews did not believe the Samaritans were of the bloodline of Israel, rather they thought they were a racially-mixed society with both Jewish and pagan ancestry. Now you know why this feud incited such deep resentment from both sides.

Jesus could have picked anyone to be the hero of this parable. By choosing a Samaritan he started the process of breaking down cultural barriers. He took this opportunity to give a visual illustration showing no matter what one calls himself or what culture of people they are born from the only way to reach the Father is through the Son. Eventually, Jesus' disciples would have to share the Gospel of Christ to people outside of the Jewish tribes. As the crowd listened to the teachings of Jesus, they needed to know everyone from all nationalities mattered to him.

"When He Saw the Man"

The Samaritan man was perfect for this rescue job for three main reasons. The first qualification found in the text is the Samaritan was a man of compassion. As Christians we are called to view the needs of those around us through the eyes and heart of Christ. In our present society it is not always easy to assess the needs of others when so many pride themselves in their ability to bury their true feelings, hiding them deep behind concrete walls while wearing a smile across their faces as if nothing is wrong at the same time. Wouldn't it be easier if we all had "thought bubbles" over our heads detailing the raw and real truth about our needs and struggles? Were this so, we might know better how to help our neighbor and our neighbor might know better how to help us.

Christmas is a wonderful time of year…a time for giving. It's the season when everyone loves others by giving to local charities, helping the needy, donating toys for tots or volunteering in the soup kitchens. As Christians, shouldn't we be walking out these actions all year long? Compassion is not just seeing a need and feeling sorry for the bearer of this burden. It is being moved to action by using your God-given gifts to intervene in the lives of others and offer help.

While driving out of my neighborhood one morning to run some errands I approached an intersection where a car had stalled blocking one lane of traffic. A steady stream of cars passed the stalled vehicle one after the other in the other lane. Waiting with my blinker on to enter the open lane I watched car after car zip past the lady sitting helplessly in the stalled vehicle. An opening in traffic eventually came and I pulled out, navigated around the other cars, and pulled in behind the stalled car. I stepped out of my car, walked to the window of her car, and asked if I could help in any way. She explained her car would start, but it would not roll forward. "It must be locked up," she said.

I am not an auto mechanic by any stretch of the imagination, but I thought I could at least help get her car out of the road. I asked her to put the gear in neutral while I pushed her car to the side of the road, clearing the blocked lane. She signaled she was ready. I heaved and grunted until I saw sparkling lights in front of my eyes but the car would not budge. I asked, "Is your foot off the brake?" She said it was. With her permission, I climbed into the car to see if I could figure out what might be the problem. The engine started right up, however when I put the car in drive it lunged but would not continue moving forward. A little light bulb turned on in my head. I looked down to see if the emergency brake was engaged. Sure enough it was. She thanked me profusely while belittling herself for such an oversight. She drove away and traffic resumed its normal flow.

There are people all around us who are struggling to move forward with their lives stifled in their attempts because they forgot to release their emergency brake. Often times it only takes one person willing to inconvenience themselves just a bit in order to help us release the brake and get moving again. We all need help at some point in our lives. Paul tells us to "Bear one another's burdens, and so fulfill the law of Christ."[12] When we help someone who is stalled in the crossroads of life, we not only keep them moving in the right direction, we keep the traffic moving for everyone traveling down the straight and narrow road.

Equipped For the Job

The second qualification found in the text is the Samaritan was a man of means. He didn't just call 911 and wait for the emergency crew to arrive. This man had with him bandages, medicine and money to offer extended care. Even if the Levite and Priest had stopped to help, they may have been ill-equipped for this victim's serious wounds. There is no mention as to the occupation of this Samaritan and no explanation as to why he carried these supplies. However, it was a good thing he packed those bandages along with the oil and wine which were commonly used during those times as antiseptic. We can speculate the Samaritan was aware of the treacherous journey and may have brought these items along for his own personal necessity. Or could it be possible he traveled this *Highway of Blood* often looking for robbery victims in need of care?

Before my band, Tinman Jones, graduated to a tour bus, we traveled in an old moving truck. It was a 16-foot box. The box was a customized walk-through to the cab, complete with wall-to-wall carpet, four bunk beds, two couches and a dresser. It was definitely a sight to see all of us streaming out of its cab each time we stopped at a gas station to refuel. We resembled the over-packed and undersized clown car driving around at the circus.

On one particular trip, the battery ran down and the engine stopped. We flagged someone down to give us a jump so we could get to the next town. We made it into town, but unfortunately, it died again. It seemed to indicate the alternator was no longer charging. The camp where we were performing that night was another 20 miles down the road and we felt the most important goal was to get to the venue.

We coasted the truck to a side street where I took the battery out and carried it to a nearby service station for a quick charge. When I returned, the others were talking to an elderly gentleman with a large frame by the name of Adolf. Adolf had a Buick with an overloaded trunk full of so many tools the rear of the car sank low to the ground. We explained our plight to Adolf. He agreed to follow us to the campground and offered his mechanic skills on site. Once at the campground, we unloaded the trailer while Adolf removed the alternator.

Once the part was removed, Adolf explained he needed to take the alternator into town so it could be tested at a parts store. To do this he also needed cash in case he needed to purchase a new part. Red flags went off in our minds as we pictured our alternator and money forever disappearing. Yet, what other choices did we have? With few options, we handed Adolf a tidy sum of green and watched him drive off into the distance as we said a prayer.

With Adolf gone, we continued preparing for the concert. Just before time to start the concert his low riding Buick came driving back down the road. The test showed the alternator was in good working order. Adolf returned every dollar with the pledge he would continue working on the truck while we played the show.

At the conclusion of the concert, we broke set and loaded the trailer. There was no sign of Adolf, no note or explanation of any kind. We didn't know if the truck was fixed or if we were stranded there for the night. With a little apprehension, we piled into the truck and turned the key. The old truck fired up and purred like a kitten. After a long night's drive we arrived safely back home. To this day we do not know what Adolf did, who he was, where he went or why he left without us being able to thank or compensate him. We praised God for our Good Samaritan who just happened to have a trunk full of tools. God knows every detail of what you need. What sometimes may seem like random assistance is actually Divine Intervention. God will always send help, well-equipped to meet your specific need and at exactly the perfect time.

The Facilitator

Not only was the Good Samaritan a man of compassion and means, but the third qualification found in the text says he had something else even more critical to his ability to provide aid to the injured man. He had a donkey! Remember, the fallen man is lying on a steep, rocky, windy and treacherous path. The Good Samaritan, in his strength alone, could not have carried the victim.

Had it not been for the donkey's contribution to the rescue, other individuals willing to pitch in and help the Samaritan would have been the man's only hope for rescue. Time was of the essence in getting the beaten man to safety. I would like to label the Samaritan's donkey a facilitator.

Facilitate means to make easier or less difficult; to help forward; to assist the progress of another. The definition of facilitator describes the key role of the Samaritan donkey. Each time this story is told the Samaritan is always praised as the hero. It is important to note he could not have helped this man had it not been for his trusty beast of burden...his donkey.

Have you ever wondered what makes your favorite actor, singer, artist or politician a celebrity? Sure, the person with their name in lights has a degree of talent. But most performing artists also have writers, publishers, managers, agents, concert promoters, sound engineers, lighting technicians, stage hands, personal assistants and the list goes on and on. Without this long list of support personnel, the star would not shine so bright.

In church circles, a pastor often gets credit when the church is doing great, and criticized when the congregation is in decline. The fact is the pastor can't carry out the mission of the church alone. It takes a team of facilitators, like you and me, to shoulder much of the load. The pastor provides leadership, direction and vision. It bothers me to hear people criticize a pastor for what they believe he isn't doing well. It makes me want to ask them, "What are doing to you help him?" Is the lack of success in a church really the pastor's fault, or could it be he is expected to do everything with little support from his congregation?

Too many church members believe the pastor is supposed to be a one-man show. They want to reap the benefits of hard work and commitment without having to do any work or give a commitment to anything themselves. When the church numbers fail to increase they are first in line to identify the pastor as the problem.

A minister friend of mine gave me some good advice during the time I served as a youth pastor. The youth group had grown consistently for a while and then it seemed as though the attendance had capped and the numbers could not be increased further. My friend shared with me something he had learned through his own experience as a pastor. "God will not allow a group or ministry to grow larger than the support team's ability to effectively minister to the group."

I have seen his advice bear truth throughout a variety of ministry opportunities. Working or serving as a one-man or woman show you will only be able to take whatever it is you are doing so far. As more facilitators are drawn into and discipled through the ministry, the greater the ministry will grow and the more people it will effectively reach. When your ministry or church is not growing like you think it should, it may not be the pastor who is not doing enough. It is more likely he is at the point where he needs additional facilitators to carry more of the burden in order to continue up the path toward accomplishing the vision God has given him.

There are also pastors who try to do everything themselves without looking for help and support from the facilitators within their congregation. Whether you are a church staff member, leader, volunteer or even a corporate "missionary" take note and remember the advice I was given by my minister friend: one person can only do so much. Most church members are willing to do something if they are asked. Many don't know how to take the initiative and volunteer or they feel uncomfortable doing so on their own. I do not see anywhere in the story of the Good Samaritan where the donkey brayed, "Hey, why don't you put the man on my back and let me carry him." The donkey was only a willing participant. The Samaritan took the initiative and used his available animal.

Are you uncomfortable asking for help? Isn't it sad how many of us would rather struggle alone waiting for someone to pass by and offer assistance rather than asking first for help. Occasionally, I get a little upset if I am obviously overloaded and I see available personnel standing around watching when they could be helping. I keep thinking, "Surely they will notice I could use a hand and will choose to come over and offer their help."

Maybe it is just my stubborn pride coupled with an unwillingness to impose on someone else's time, but too often I keep struggling along by myself rather than giving someone else an opportunity to help me. As I look back on all the times I did ask for help, I can't remember a single time I was ever turned down.

Generally, when asked for help people are willing to do what they can. They may just lack the initiative or creativity to volunteer on their own. I encourage you to engage available facilitators to carry a part of the load. Most of the time they will appreciate the blessing that comes from the opportunity to help you complete the task.

Every time you commit yourself to serve in a ministry, whether inside or outside of the church, you become a facilitator of that ministry. You play an important role in helping it move forward by creating an environment where others desire to get involved. When you stop and help others carry a heavy load, whether or not you ever receive any credit for doing so, you are engaging in the ministry of a facilitator just like the Good Donkey. When you give of yourself willingly to help others, your Father in heaven sees your efforts and will place His favor on your shoulders.

Jesus teaches us in the book of Matthew to "take heed that you do not do your charitable deeds before men, to be seen by them. Otherwise you have no reward from your Father in heaven. Therefore, when you do a charitable deed, do not sound a trumpet before you as the hypocrites do in the synagogues and in the streets, that they may have glory from men. Assuredly, I say to you, they have their reward. But when you do a charitable deed, do not let your left hand know what your right hand is doing, that your charitable deed may be in secret; and your Father who sees in secret will Himself reward you openly."[13]

Whatever you do, work at it with all your might, and do it all for the Glory of the Lord. Your efforts will not go unnoticed; God sees and knows the motives of your heart. Continually look for ways to be a facilitator. Don't get so focused on the demands in your daily journey that you pass by someone lying alone and in need on the other side of the road you travel.

Chapter 3
Between Death and the Lion

The Bible is full of stories which seem to get overshadowed by the favorite Sunday school lessons. The favorites are great, but there are some equally inspiring stories never getting the attention they deserve. 1 Kings 13 tells an amazing story I have never heard taught or preached. Let's first look at the events leading up to our next donkey story.

David, a man after God's own heart, followed the Lord all of his days and God promised David his kingdom would be established forever. Then along came Solomon, David's son, who followed in his father's footsteps for a time and then started allowing idol worship into his kingdom. Solomon had many foreign wives and concubines and as a result many of these women brought their pagan beliefs into his kingdom which eventually took its toll on Solomon. The book of 1 Kings reveals he amassed a collection of 700 wives and 300 concubines. Eventually, he was influenced by these foreign religions and drifted away from the one true God. A quick-witted friend of mine once joked, "Solomon's many wives were so he could come home and find at least one in a good mood."

God became angry with Solomon and decided to strip much of the kingdom from him. He sent His prophet, Ahijah, to meet a mighty young man, a servant of Solomon, named Jeroboam. He told Ahijah to tell Jeroboam God was going to make him king over ten tribes of Israel. The prophesy proclaimed if Jeroboam would walk in the ways of the Lord just as David did all of his days God would see to it his kingdom would also be established forever. Solomon heard of this and sought to kill Jeroboam, who fled to Egypt where he remained until Solomon died. When Solomon died, Rehoboam, Solomon's son, was anointed King in his place.

Rehoboam did not exercise the wisdom of his father, taking counsel from his young peers instead of listening to the counsel of the wise elders. He imposed harsh taxes and burdens upon Israel. His actions led to the decision made by the ten tribes to pull out of Israel and anoint Jeroboam as their King.

One of King Jeroboam's first acts as King was to set up golden calves, one in Bethel and one in the tribe of Dan. He also set up high places where the people could worship, so they wouldn't travel to Jerusalem and risk persuasion to rejoin the allegiance of Rehoboam.

Keep in mind, just a short time before becoming king, God told Jeroboam if he would follow Him, his kingdom would established forever. Immediately, he throws everything God said out of the window and sets up idol worship. It is amazing to me how many kings over Israel had the same opportunity and yet turned a deaf ear to the promise of God. We all should take careful note here; when you follow the ways of the Lord He establishes your steps and His promises become reality in your life.

The Man of God is Sent

God sends a "Man of God" from Judah to Bethel where Jeroboam was offering incense on his newly constructed altar. We do not know exactly where in Judah he was from, but if we assumed he was from Jerusalem, as he very well may have been, then the journey from Jerusalem to Bethel would have been about ten miles north. When this man of God approached Jeroboam, he prophesied against the altar and said it would be split apart and its ashes dumped out. This angered the new king of the ten tribes of Israel, and in his rage he reached out his hand toward the man of God and shouted to his guards, "Arrest him!" Immediately, his hand withered and he could not pull it back down. At the same moment, the altar split in two and the ashes spilled out, just as the man of God had prophesied.

Jeroboam cried out in repentance to the man of God and his hand was restored. To show gratitude and further repentance, Jeroboam invited God's prophet to come to his house so he could feed him and put him up for the night. The man of God replied, "If you were to give me half your house, I would not go in with you, nor would I eat bread nor drink water in this place. For the Lord commanded me that I should not eat bread, nor drink water, nor return by the same way I came."[14] This instruction from God is key to the story because it shows God was very specific to this man of God. It says he went another way and did not return by the way he came to Bethel, just as he had been instructed by the Lord.

Enter the Old Prophet

There also happened to be an elderly prophet living at Bethel, which is not surprising because, even though Bethel is the new house of idolatry in Israel, it is historically a holy place. Both Abraham and Jacob built altars to God here and during the time of the judges, the Ark of the Covenant was housed in Bethel. I find it disappointing there is a king setting up idol worship and leading the people away from God with a prophet of God silently living nearby and without protest.

His sons were either participants in the sacrifices of idolatry, or at least spectators, for they saw the events between the man of God and the king. They told their father, the prophet, all about this man of God confronting the idolatry and the old prophet had to go meet him. He saddled his donkey and headed out on a path to intercept the man of God.

The old prophet found the man of God resting under an oak tree and invited him to come home with him for the night. The man of God informed the old prophet of God's instructions and promptly declined the invitation. The old prophet replied, "Oh, I am a prophet like you and an angel came to me and told me to bring you to my house." The scripture tells us this old prophet was lying to the man of God.

You have to stop and wonder why a prophet would lie to another prophet and make him go against a command of the Lord. Maybe he just wanted to get the first-hand gossip from a fellow prophet. It may have been years since this old prophet had been used by God and he wanted to feel the anointing again by being around an anointed man of God. Maybe the devil came to him as an "angel of light" and deceived him to get to the man of God.

When you have heard from God, and you know what He has commanded you to do, be very careful about taking a contrary word from someone else. This man of God should have counseled with God himself and asked, "Lord, is this true? Did you change your mind? Am I to go with him?" He made no such query of the Lord. He blindly turned aside at the word of another.

Obedience to God is required of all who follow Him. Many men in the Bible lost out with God because they did not obey; rather they acted according to their own rational thinking. The man of God let his guard down when he was in the presence of a fellow prophet. We can never let our guard down when it comes to absolute obedience to God or to His Word. This man of God from Judah learned the hard way, for when they arrived at the old prophet's house; God really did speak through the old prophet to the man of God telling him, because of his disobedience, he would not make it home alive.

A Fallen Man of God

The man of God finishes his meal and the old prophet lets him take his donkey for the remainder of the trip. The donkey is saddled and the man of God departs. Not far down the road a lion pounces out and kills the man of God and stands by the corpse of the prophet. Strangely, the donkey also remains, standing by the fallen prophet with the lion. Can you picture the scene as if you were one of the passersby on the road? There is a man lying dead on the side of the road with a lion and a donkey standing side by side and next to him.

It must have been quite a sight to see, because men started telling this story around the town until news came to the old prophet. The old prophet, after hearing the story, concluded this must have been the prophet from Judah and he rode out and found the man with the donkey and the lion still standing there. He brought the prophet's body back and gave him a proper burial.

The Brave Donkey

Upon reading such an incredible story I could not get the scene out of my head of a donkey standing there, between a lion and his fresh kill. The bravery of the donkey amazed me and I had to discover more about why he seemed to show no fear. An average donkey stands about 50 inches tall and weighs roughly 450 pounds. A typical lion has a height of about 40 inches at the shoulders and sports a weight of around 400 pounds, making the lion and donkey close to the same size. It would have made perfect sense for the donkey to bolt and get safely out of harms way while braying to the prophet, "You're on your own, Bub!"

One of the jobs for which donkeys are commonly employed is to guard sheep, goats and other livestock. Donkeys have been known to fight off wolves and coyotes and can be quite formidable fighters. They are instinctively protective over the animals they are placed with and will defend them unto death if necessary.

Shortly after Terri and I were married we moved into a rental home. The rental was the second house from the end of the street and two houses down from the railroad tracks. It usually was not a big issue when the train came roaring by; you just had to wait until it passed to continue a conversation. One night we were awakened in the early morning hours by a loud crashing sound. It was completely dark in the room and we couldn't see anything. The bed was shaking and debris was flying around the room. The first thought racing through our minds was a train had derailed and was barreling through our bedroom as we lay helpless in the dark. We sat up in bed and I instinctively threw my arm over Terri as though I could stop a train to save my wife. Our hearts were racing and both of us were screaming at the top of our lungs, "Aaaahhhhhhh, Aaaaaaaaaaahhhhhh, AAAAAAAAHHHHHHHHHH!!!"

When the dust settled, the bed stopped shaking and no more crashing was heard, I reached up and clicked on a light to get a first glance at the disaster zone. I found it was not a train at all. The wall opposite the foot of the bed was home to my study desk and just above the desk was a stack of shelves I had assembled. They came equipped with slotted railing where brackets are inserted so shelving can lie across it. You probably have some in your house, and if you do, I recommend you not allow it to support a collection of Bible reference books, a Strong's Exhaustive Concordance, an entire set of encyclopedias and various other books and references.

One side of these shelves was anchored securely into a stud, while the other side was just screwed into the dry wall. In the middle of that fateful night the weak side pulled out of the wall and the entire shelving structure swung out, hinged on the anchored side, and dumped all of these books as it went until at last there were no more books remaining to fall. The wooden shelves found a resting place somewhere between the desk and the bed.

It is funny to reflect on our actions during a crisis once the moment of panic has passed, and needless to say, my attempt to protect Terri from the oncoming train let her know I would do anything to keep her safe. Instinctive bravery is the character I believe this donkey demonstrated when the lion pounced upon the prophet, knocking him to the ground. Do you know why the lion stopped short of completing its attack? It's likely the lion instinctively knew what a donkey was capable of doing, and as long as the donkey stood there, the lion was unable to devour his fresh kill.

I find comfort in reading these words in 2 Timothy, "For God has not given us a spirit of fear, but of power and of love and of a sound mind."[15] There are over 100 times in the Bible where we read statements such as, "Do not fear" or "Do not be afraid." It can't be an accident for God to include such reassurance so many times in His Word, it must be a concept in which He wants us to pay attention. He wants us to be as brave as donkeys as we walk through life, and not succumb to fear when life takes a disastrous turn.

A farmer was interviewing candidates for a new farm hand and one particular young man seemed to be the most impressive. There was, however, a phrase on the young man's resume the old farmer found odd. It read: "I can sleep when the wind blows." Even though the farmer thought it was an odd thing to put on a resume, everything else about the man checked out and he offered the young man the job.

The farmer was quite impressed with the new hand's work ethic and ability to handle any task given to him. One night, the farmer was awakened by a tremendous storm. He jumped out of bed to take actions to secure the farm. He first stopped by the farm hand's quarters to enlist his help but the young man would not awake. No amount of calling, shaking or rolling could interrupt his slumber. Angrily, the farmer stomped outside vowing to deal with him in the morning.

He rushed to the barn to secure the doors and found they were already barred shut. Then off he rushed to the hay to find a tarp draped over and staked down. The farmer continued to various areas finding all tools and supplies put away. All the animals were in safe areas and all loose objects were secured.

It was then the words of the resume came to him, "I can sleep when the wind blows." It was clear the young man took care of these things every day so when the storm raged, he did not have to be alarmed because he had done everything he could do. The rest was in God's hands.

We can neither predict nor prevent most of the storms from blowing into our lives, but if we will do every day all we can do to secure our lives and then trust the rest into God's hands, we can sleep when the wind blows. We can be brave and fear not, believing "we have done all, to stand."[16] When you have done everything that you can do, stand tall, be brave and be strong, allowing God to turn fear into power, love and a sound mind.

My son was born under a slew of miraculous circumstances. I was conducting a youth event in our city and my wife Terri was at home taking care of our young daughter. She was about two weeks from her anticipated due date. Terri's mother, both a nurse and great woman of God, had an overwhelming feeling she needed to drive the hour and a half to our home for an unscheduled visit. When she examined Terri, she sensed something was not right and took Terri to see the doctor immediately. There were indeed complications and the call came for me to get to the hospital quickly. Jamin was delivered just 15 minutes after I arrived at the hospital. He had fluid in his lungs and was put under an oxygen tent where he remained for four days before they discovered a hole in his heart.

He was then air-lifted to a nearby Children's Hospital. We drove up the next morning for an early meeting with the surgeon who told us the hole was the least of his problems. Jamin also had an underdeveloped aorta with a gap in it above the heart. The doctor explained there is a vessel which bypasses the baby's lungs when in the mother's womb. In most babies it dissolves within twenty-four hours after birth, but in Jamin's case this vessel was still open five days later. This was significant because this vessel was also bypassing the gap in the aorta charged with supplying blood to his tiny body. The doctor remarked, "I can't explain why this vessel hasn't disappeared, but it is what is keeping him alive." I could hardly keep from shouting, "I know why!"

The story is much longer, but the main point I want to get to is, through this entire and great trial I kept seeing signs God's hand was at work. Even though the events were traumatic and wrenching, I had an unexplainable calm, strength and confidence everything was going to be fine. I could not have navigated such a storm had it not been for God replacing potential fear with the brave heart of a donkey. The lion was roaring, but I was able to stand and let God do His work. Jamin has become an amazing man of God in his own right, and his testimony has helped many others weathering a storm.

When you face the storms in your life and lions are roaring threats against you, take up the heart of a donkey, and stand brave and tall. Do not be afraid; trust in God who will never fail to deliver you.

The Lost Art of Loyalty

Like everyone, I certainly have my share of weaknesses. Yet, I also have my strengths and if I were to name just one of them it would definitely be loyalty. Once you are my friend, you are stuck with me for life. I have the same insurance agent I started with years ago, and I like being a long-term patron of a business. I don't change my cell service carrier each time my contract runs out and I support my pastor and church with everything in me.

I look around today and find loyalty seems to be a fading art in the world. People quickly change alliances based on what is in their best interest for the moment and commitment is nothing more than a word in the dictionary. If a relationship isn't what you expected, end it and find another. If your kids are not turning out right, disown them. If a pastor or church makes a mistake, find another. When things don't go your way you can turn on your friends, your employer or your country and it seems perfectly normal in our modern culture.

In this story, I see a great sense of loyalty in this donkey, even though the donkey did not even belong to this man of God. They had just met when the old prophet saddled the donkey and handed the reigns to the prophet from Judah. The donkey would have been justified to have walked away braying, "This isn't my master. There is no reason for me to stick my neck out for him." It could have thought, "Well, he's dead. Nothing more I can do here so I might as well find someone else to serve." Nope, not this donkey! He had been given a job to do and he was loyal to the end.

Remember the scene in *"Forrest Gump"* when he was in Vietnam and his unit was under attack. He remembered the words of Jenny, "Run Forrest!" Forrest ran as fast as he could to get out of harm's way. When he realized his best friend, Bubba, was not with him he ran back into the firefight to find Bubba. Along the way he would find other fallen soldiers who he carried to safety one at a time. After each one he brought out, he ran back into the battle zone to find Bubba. The actions of Forrest Gump represent a valuable type of loyalty not simply the typical convenience-based, self-serving loyalty we see so prevalent today.

Before I sound too harsh about today's society I admit fleeting loyalty isn't a new problem. Jesus called his disciples out by name to follow Him. They witnessed miracles, heard great teaching and even experienced the prestige of being associated with Jesus. Then when Jesus was taken into custody, beaten and hung on a cross, at the very time he needed them most, they scattered, each one going back to what they were doing before they were called. They had fully invested in Jesus, giving him their loyalty until it didn't work out like they thought it should. Then, they went a different way.

David had an impressive sense of loyalty to the call of God and to the anointing, not only in his life, but to others. When he was running from King Saul he had two opportunities to kill him and take his place as king, but his loyalty to the anointing of God would not allow unfaithful action.

I have a secret to tell you not many people know. Pastors are not perfect and neither are church people. Someone stopped me in a restaurant and told me about a church member who made them a promise and then did not keep their word. They were left disappointed in the whole church and not sure they even wanted to attend there any longer.

Their disappointment was legitimate to the point they really were in need of reconciliation. When the person they were counting on did not follow through on their promise my friend was left with ill feelings toward this individual. It does appear to me they were taking their feelings to the extreme and showing a lack of both patience and loyalty by considering the possibility of writing off an entire congregation due to one person's mistake. If a church has to be perfect and the pastor flawless before one can attend, then every sanctuary should remain empty.

A person who nitpicks and brings to light every flaw from pastor to church member should spend a little more time reading God's word. In fact the Apostle Paul tells us we need to live our lives "Bearing with one another, and forgiving one another, if anyone has a complaint against another; even as Christ forgave you, so you also must do."[17] The phrase "bearing with one another" is literally translated as "overlooking the undesirable traits of others." If every church member in a congregation could grasp the meaning of this verse, it would revolutionize the relationships within the church. By showing greater loyalty to one another and choosing to ignore what is disliked about another it gives us the opportunity to focus on what we share in common. When we look for and believe the best in others we are better able to love them with the perfect love of God.

It has to start with someone, so be a person who will be loyal to your church and pastor. Stand by it, defend it, go down with it if necessary. Don't be the first person to bail out at the first sign of a storm. Be loyal to your faith by refusing to be like the "one tossed to and fro and carried about with every wind of doctrine, by the trickery of men, in the cunning craftiness of deceitful plotting."[18] Be the one your family and friends can count on, through thick and thin, good times and bad, just as the donkey who stood loyally beside the fallen prophet.

And Going, and Going, and Going...

Remember the pink battery bunny with the motto...just keeps going and going and going...? The original trophy for tenacity would have to go to the donkey facing off with the lion. We do not know how long it stood there by the lion; possibly days. Remember the men who passed by and saw the donkey standing by the lion? They traveled to town and told the story. Word finally made it to the old prophet who assumed what had happened and journeyed by foot to where the man of God had fallen. The donkey was still there, standing by the corpse of the man of God and the lion.

On one of our Tinman Jones tours, our bus broke down along a lonely road in Tennessee. We were headed to Cleveland for a two-night youth convention and then on to a series of other concerts. We had an unwritten policy never to miss a commitment no matter what it took to keep it. Therefore, we called for a very large tow truck and phoned our mechanic, who fortunately was willing to make road calls for us and drove to Tennessee to work on our bus. When he arrived he determined the bus would take a couple of days to repair, which was unacceptable but necessary, whether we liked it or not. This news was absolutely not what we wanted to hear.

The lot we were towed to also rented Budget trucks which gave us an idea. We rented a truck, emptied our trailer of everything we needed and stacked this equipment into the truck. Then we took mattresses off of the bunks in the bus and layered the remaining floor space of the truck with them and finished loading up. Two of us road in the cab and the rest laid on the mattresses in the box of the truck. In hindsight it might not have been the brightest or safest idea, but we had a show to perform so off to Cleveland we went, stacked like furniture on a cross-country move. Did I mention it was November? Cleveland isn't known for its warm November climate and already had snow on the ground. The bus repair took more than just a couple of days and we ended up traveling to a weeks' worth of concerts for what we have since affectionately dubbed as the "Budget Truck Tour." This kind of unrelenting devotion to see the job to completion through danger or adversity is also the kind of commitment I see in this tenacious donkey.

There are many unsung heroes in our ranks who have taught Bible classes for years, spent a lifetime on the mission field or other ministries and service to God where they have proved faithful through good times and hard times. I was greatly inspired by a friend of mine, Joe Murphy, who had a vision and heart to start a

Royal Ranger group in our church. He had a real passion for those boys to be mentored through a successful Royal Ranger ministry and for years struggled with finding leaders to help who would be faithful. The group seemed to struggle with little support. Attendance was poor and leaders were scarce. Joe, even though discouraged many times, would not relent or give up on the vision he felt God had given him. I was so excited when a few years ago things started to come together with some men who seemed to catch Joe's vision and boys started to get excited about the program. Now the group is doing wonderful things in our church because one man remained faithful.

It would be easy, even understandable, to walk away when you are standing between death and a lion. On one hand there is no evidence of life or reason to continue, and on the other side forces are poised to devour you. When God has given you a vision or a heart for something, do not let go or give up on it. Too many people give up one step from victory and just short of seeing the fulfillment of the promises of God.

Paul said in his letter to the Philippians, "I thank my God upon every remembrance of you, always in every prayer of mine making request for you all with joy, for your fellowship in the Gospel from the first day until now, being confident of this very thing, that He who has begun a good work in you will complete it until the day of Jesus Christ."[19]

Write this down as a promise on which you can stand. When God gives you a work to do, He is going to complete what He has begun. God does not leave unfinished business. When you think no progress is being made know God is still on the scene in ways you may not even see, and the work is still moving forward. It may get hard at times, but Paul wrote in his letter to the Galatians, "Let us not grow weary while doing good; for in due season we shall reap if we do not lose heart."[20]

Keep your chin up and your eyes ahead, you may be standing between death and the lion, but God will complete His work through you if you don't lose heart. Be brave, loyal and tenacious just as this donkey was, and you will see great fruit grow from your labor.

Chapter 4
The Lost Donkeys

Kish was a mighty man from the tribe of Benjamin. He had a son named Saul who was the most handsome man in all of Israel, not to mention one of the tallest, standing roughly a head taller than the average man. The book of I Samuel tells of a time when Kish lost his entire herd or pace of donkeys. A man's wealth was measured by how many donkeys and livestock he possessed making this loss even more tragic. Losing such prized animals diminished his wealth considerably and lowered his status in the community. Kish called for his son, Saul, and tasked him with finding the lost donkeys.

Saul and a trusted servant set out on this important mission with singleness in purpose and a heart of determination. Saul understood the importance of returning the lost donkeys. His search led him through the mountains of Ephraim all the way to the land of Shalisha, yet sadly the donkeys were not found. The path continued beyond Shaalim, through the land of the Benjamites, but the lost animals were not located. Once they reached a region called Zuph, Saul concerned his father might be worried about their long absence, suggested they return empty-handed. However, the servant had one last idea. He knew of a man of God in a nearby city who was believed to know all things. Therefore, he suggested they ask this man of God if he could tell them where the donkeys might have wandered.

This man of God was the prophet Samuel. Samuel had received a message from God the night before saying he would meet a man from the tribe of Benjamin and he was to anoint this man, "Commander over My people Israel." As Saul approached Samuel, Samuel informed Saul the donkeys had in fact safely returned home on their own. Samuel then invited the two men to stay for a feast. During the evening meal Samuel revealed to Saul he was to be the first King of Israel. Saul thought he was on a mission to find a pace of lost donkeys; however, what he found was the plan God had ordained for his life.

I really don't like losing things. One of life's biggest mysteries is *where tiny objects disappear to when they are dropped*. Sometimes, when working on a gadget of some kind, I'll drop a small screw onto the floor. Instantly, it vanishes into the abyss where it can't be found. I will get down on my hands and knees and pat every inch of a quarter-mile radius yet still not find the dropped screw. This phenomenon ranks right up there with the dryer sock perplexity. As I read the story, I can feel the mounting frustration as Saul looks high and low across five lands for these wandering beasts only to discover they had already headed back toward their home pasture.

Bravo was a beautiful Border Collie with all the characteristic markings of his breed. Border Collies are free range dogs with one of the highest IQ's of any variety of canines. His desire to roam the wide-open spaces of Arkansas was squelched by our town's leash law and our small backyard. As Bravo grew, he became quite the escape artist; his abilities were right up there with Houdini. The backyard was not enough to curb his desire to run free in our strict "leash-law" city. I had to build a 10 X 15-foot pen, six feet in height to thwart his escape when family members were not available to supervise his activities. To our dismay, we found we had a dog that could climb a six foot, chain link fence like it was a handy staircase. This forced me to lace a chain link top across the span of the enclosure so he could not launch himself to freedom under the cover of darkness.

Even the custom roof proved to be insufficient to stifle his drive to roam the city like Tramp in the famed movie. Often, after Bravo escaped, we found an exploited weakness in the pen cover with a tuft of black and white fur marking the point of his escape.

One time, Bravo escaped enjoying a several day adventure. We combed the neighborhood, calling out his name over and over again, but there was no trace of our beloved pet. Fortunately, our phone number was inscribed on the tag hanging from his collar. People from all around the city called telling us how they petted our friendly Collie long enough to read our number before Bravo bolted and disappeared yet again.

Finally, someone recognized the importance of holding on to him until we could get to the location and retrieve our wayward adventurer. As we reflected on the locations from which we had received calls it was clear Bravo made a wide circle around the entire city. His total journey spanned at least ten miles yet he was secured only a half-mile from home. I figure he was headed home to get some food and rest up before taking his next expedition.

The donkeys belonging to Kish must have had the same sense of adventure as did our beloved Bravo. They returned home safely on their own after a brief adventure. It is obvious the donkeys were not the ones who were lost, but rather it was Saul who was lost and in search for God's plan for his life. As I studied the lands Saul traveled looking for his father's donkeys, I saw many similarities between Saul's search and the way we search for God's will in our own lives. Let's take a trip with Saul and see what we discover.

Passing through the Mountains of Ephraim

The scripture says Saul first passed through Ephraim. Ephraim was largely uncultivated hill country to the northeast of Jerusalem, between the central towns and the Jordan Valley. Mount Ephraim was the historical name given to the mountainous district of Palestine occupied by the tribe of Ephraim.[21] This land extended from Bethel to the plain of Jezreel. Around this time these hills were densely wooded, intersected by well watered, fertile valleys. This rugged countryside is the area where Joshua was buried.[22]

Do you remember the rush of youthful emotions you experienced when you graduated from high school? I sure do. On one hand, I felt the relief of completing years of study, yet on the other hand I was overwhelmed by the need to discover what I was going to do with my future.

As a Christian teen, I was keenly aware of the responsibility to find God's will for my life and then pursue His calling. For me, locating the anointed path felt like Ponce de Leon searching for the fountain of youth. After a while I questioned if it even existed.

Times of new discovery can be compared to traveling through Ephraim's mountainous, untamed land embodied by deep, thick forests. Whether fresh out of high school, college or as a new believer, the first experiences in discovering God's will for our lives are often quite the adventure.

One of my friends loves looking for treasure, geocaching, and participating in anything leading to the discovery of a red 'X' on an old map. One day while looking through some old county maps he found a town on the map which, as far as he knew, no longer existed. After some research, he discovered this was a depot town on a stretch of railway and at one time in history it functioned as a bustling little community.

My friend called me and asked if I was interested in searching alongside him for this town. He said, "We'll take a metal detector along and see what we can dig up." It sounded like a fun adventure to me so without hesitation I said, "I'm in." Off we went with copies of the old maps to guide us to our treasure. The railway was a great point of reference. We parked the car near the track and headed down the double steel path following each contour of the track closely to the spot where the station should have been located.

We found a curve in the railroad in the precise spot where the settled town once stood. Our hearts were racing. No structure remained, but you could see in the lay of the land where the main road cut through and where buildings once stood. It was surreal to think we were standing in the middle of a town where people once worked and lived but was today just a memory reduced to markings on an old county map.

We followed the road a bit and then branched out into the wooded area to see what we could find. Very soon we were lost in the deep underbrush of the forest. I have a decent sense of direction, however on this day I was completely turned around. I had no idea which direction led back to the train tracks. Fortunately, I remembered some scouting skills I learned as a boy and the time had come to put them into action. Knowing what time of day it was, all I had to do was look at the sun to get my bearing and we would be back on track in a snap. I looked up to find not a single peep of sunlight through the clouded sky. Technique number one failed miserably. Not to be discouraged, I told my friend all we had to do was find some trees with moss on them and we would know which way was north. Every survivalist knows moss grows on the north side of a tree.

Once we found a mossy tree it was obvious someone forgot to tell the moss on what side of the tree it was supposed to grow. There was moss growing on the trees full circumference. One by one, my directional discovery plans fell through.

My friend however, came up with a brilliant plan to call another friend asking him to drive to the location where we parked and honk his horn so we could follow the sound. The trouble with his plan was we were too far into the woods for our signal to reach the cell phone tower. It would have worked, I'm sure, if we'd had at least one bar of cell service. Our final plan was to walk a straight path hoping we would come out somewhere. We eventually popped out on the tracks and followed them back to civilization.

God's plan for our lives can sometimes feel very cryptic. We often find ourselves searching for clues along the journey. Have you ever felt like the clues you find offer more questions than answers? I love a line from the movie *National Treasure*. Throughout the movie the team navigated from one clue to another. It seemed the treasure was not discoverable because each clue resulted in finding another riddle. The character Riley sighs under his breath, "Why don't they just say, 'Go here and find the treasure. Spend it wisely.'"[23] In the same way, we sometimes find ourselves impatient with God. Have you ever prayed as I have, "Lord, I want to find and follow your perfect will for my life. Just tell me in an audible voice what it is and I will do it?"

We learn from the Mountains of Ephraim, searching for God's will strengthens and equips us with everything needed to do God's will. In the Gospel of John just before Jesus made His triumphal entry into Jerusalem, we read where Jesus retreated to Ephraim because the Jews were plotting to kill him. He knew before the time of his fulfillment transpired he had to build up his strength. His day of atonement for the sins of all mankind was very near. Into this same wilderness where Saul began his search for the lost donkeys, Jesus retreated to find strength so he could complete the will of his Father.[24]

Paul, in the book of Hebrews, admonishes us saying, "Therefore do not cast away your confidence, which has great reward. For you have need of endurance, so that after you have done the will of God, you may receive the promise."[25] God not only has a perfect plan for your life, He also knows the perfect time to reveal and carry out His plan. Often times, the most challenging season we must walk through is that time of searching and waiting. However it is through this season God gives His clarity and confidence for the next part of our life's journey.

As much as I may want to, I can't just jump out of bed in the morning and decide I'm going to climb Mt. Everest by the end of the day. Great preparation, training, research and acquired skills are required if I am to survive the perilous journey and reach the summit. Likewise, by spending time in the rugged wilderness called Ephraim, you will gain the endurance and strength to find and follow the will of God for your life. Keep pressing forward.

The Land of Shalisha

The second area Saul targeted while searching for his lost donkeys was the land of Shalisha. This land is believed to be the same district of Baal-shalisha mentioned in 2 Kings 4:42, lying about twelve miles north of Lydda and west of Joppa. According to early writings, it is believed fruits ripened earlier at Baal-shalisha than anywhere else in Palestine and was called "The Land of First Fruits," a place of early opportunity.

After spending time in the wilderness on our parallel quest to find the will of God, we come out feeling stronger and better equipped to conquer the world for Christ. It is important, as we enthusiastically prepare to launch new ministries or start new causes, we do not ignore or disregard the leading of the Holy Spirit. Enthusiasm is both a powerful and driving force. However, it has both the potential to lead us in a positive direction or down a path of destruction.

In the book of Acts we find a group of enthusiastic exorcists who wanted to start a deliverance ministry for the oppressed. They had witnessed the Apostle Paul cast demons out of those possessed by tormenting spirits. With great enthusiasm they tried to cast out an evil spirit by saying, "We exorcise you by the power of Jesus whom Paul preaches." The evil spirits recognized the exorcists were powerless in their efforts and jumped on them and sent them away naked.[26]

Several years ago there was a group of students at a well-known Bible college who felt an urgency to share the message of Christ. They made the decision to leave college and start other ministries believing they were wasting their time in school while people without Christ were dying. Several years passed during which time many of them left the ministry and sadly some decided to no longer serve God. How could people with such enthusiasm for God fall so short in following His call? They fell short because they did not take the time to adequately prepare to fulfill the ministry to which God had called them.

During my mid-teen years, my family piled into a motor home and set out on a two-week trip. Our vacation included stops at Disney World, Washington D.C. and Niagara Falls. It was quite a long distance to travel on a two-week vacation.

My dad never met a stranger and could strike up a conversation with just about anyone. While in Niagara Falls, he met a local grounds keeper who told him everything he knew about Chokecherry trees. Many of these trees were in the area surrounding our camper. The man told my dad Chokecherries make great jelly. So, my parents thought it would be great fun to pick a vast supply of Chokecherries and make homemade jelly together. Everyone knows cherries are red, right? Not so with this variety. Chokecherries are ripe when they reach a dark brown color.

We quickly set out to pick all the dark brown cherries we could find. When other tourists in the area saw us picking the fruit they joined the action. It was fun to watch them naturally choose the bright red ones. They popped these red cherries into their mouths and made the most awful faces we had ever seen. What they didn't know is the bright red cherries explain where they get their name "Choke" cherry. The sweetest and most usable of this variety of cherries are the ones who have matured just a little longer and are a dark maroon, almost brown in color.

Many people pursue a dangerous method to find the will of God. I call it the "open door policy." It is when someone says, "Lord, when I see an open door I'll just assume you put it there for me to walk through." This practice can lead to one walking through any available door just because it's open. A door can be wide open in front of you, yet not opened by God. If the open door was not opened by God, then you certainly should not enter. Likewise, sometimes God may point you toward a door that is closed and He intends for you to open it yourself and walk through. Maturity is having the patience to wait for the right door, God's door, to open before you walk through it. Be willing to "Rest in the Lord, and wait patiently for Him; Do not fret because of him who prospers in his way..."[27]

God will reveal His purpose for you at exactly the right time, be careful not to let impatience get the best of you. Don't get in a hurry like the people who grabbed a hand full of bright red Chokecherries to eat only to find they were not ripened and bitter in taste. It may leave a sour taste in your mouth for years to come. Remaining patient for the cherries to ripen renders a sweet-flavored jelly, and when tasted is well worth the wait. Learn to wait upon the Lord. He knows where you need to be and when you will arrive at your ultimate destination.

Searching in Shaalim

Saul leaves the land of first fruits to comb the third area where he will search for his donkeys...the land of Shaalim. The exact location of Shaalim is unknown. Most scholars refer to this region as Shaalbim, a town in the territory of Dan where Amorites lived and paid tribute. The name Shaalim means "foxes."

Usually when we think of foxes, words like "sly," "crafty" and "wise" come to mind. As we move into the third stage to finding God's will for our lives we have completed our time in the wilderness. Because we may have been burned a few times or picked some fruit to eat before it was ripe and ready, we are definitely more experienced and wise.

In this stage of our search we seek God's will by analyzing everything. We often eagerly complete the latest ministry assessment to help us discover what ministry best suits our personality profile. We may read books like "Six Steps to Finding God's will," followed by "Ten Steps to Finding God's Will." Some of us may spend hundreds of dollars to attend seminars and workshops giving us all the angles to help us find the "Perfect Will of God" for our lives.

Zophar thought he knew something about wisdom. There sat Job on an ash heap having lost everything. While scratching his boils and listening to his wife's nagging, his friend Zophar sat down beside him and asked, "Can you search out the deep things of God? Can you find out the limits of the almighty?"[28] He makes a few more wise statements then tells Job all the calamity

Job is experiencing is because of Job's sin. In the end God made Zophar give Job an apology. As a part of his apology Zophar says, "For an empty-headed man will be wise, when a wild donkey's colt is born a man."[29] When Zophar chose to operate in his own wisdom he landed the label "empty-headed."

In November of 1985, my good friend and I went on a camping trip in the Ouachita Mountains above Hot Springs, Arkansas. Not many people camp in the mountains in November. We had the campgrounds mostly to ourselves, with the exception of a leftover hippy in a Volkswagen mini-van parked nearby, and yes, it was painted with sunflowers. We thought it would be fun to take an all-day hike around part of the lake and soon after arriving we set out on this adventure.

Lake Ouachita is a valley lake in the mountains. It has an irregular shape with many lake-filled fingers flowing around the outskirts of the hilly region. On our way back we decided to save some time so we would arrive back to our campsite early. Rather than following the contour of the lake, we opted to take a short-cut over the mountain leading back the camp.

We got out the compass we brought with us, took a reading, drew a bead and proceeded in a deliberate direction. We had a great time walking and talking until we pulled out the compass to check our orientation. The compass revealed we were off course by about 30 degrees. This could not be correct, after all, we had walked in a straight line. We decided to go a little further on our pre-established course before checking the compass again. We were now about 60 degrees off course.

My friend is a smart fellow who loves physics and has a vast library of facts stored in his brain just for fun. He concluded the problem was the iron content in the mountain affected the compass causing it to give a falsified reading. I agreed the explanation seemed reasonable. We had not deviated from our straight-line walk while on our established route.

With new information in hand we decided to disregard the compass and continue in our established direction. We've all heard stories about people walking in circles in the forest. I had never experienced it first hand until this trip when on our hike we happened upon some familiar landmarks. After a few hours walking and talking, we were once again at the very same location where we had begun our short cut. We had just hiked full circle. After a big laugh, we re-plotted our course. We committed this time to following the compass exactly. By trusting the compass we arrived back at our camp, but much later than we had hoped.

Solomon was a wise man when he wrote, "Trust in the Lord with all your heart, and do not lean on your own understanding. In all your ways acknowledge Him, and He will make straight your paths."[30] Remember, God's will for your life may not initially make perfect sense to you, your family or your friends. However, when God confirms His will in your life, you can be sure He will direct your path. Your job is to keep your eye on the compass rather than putting your trust in your own intellect.

The Land of the Benjamites

Saul had to be tired at this point. He had walked through the Mountains of Ephraim, the land of Shalisha, those first fruits, and then passed through the land of Shaalim. Next, he passes through the land of the Benjamites, and since we know Saul is a Benjamite, we see he has come back close to home and familiar territory.

This is the fourth area of significance in our quest to find and follow God's will in our lives. We've put the confusion of the wilderness behind us, our passion and zeal during the time of first fruit has waned and trying to figure out the will of God through our own wisdom has left us exhausted. At this point it seems the sensible thing to do is settle on doing whatever is comfortable for us.

When we reach this point we've often grown tired from the journey and sometimes pray, "God, I'll do what you want me to do, say what you want me to say, be what you want me to be, as long as I can do it from my living room." After all, we have responsibilities with our job, family, t-ball practice or whatever the activities of life may be. Following God's will becomes subject to our schedule. If an opportunity does come along for us to serve in ministry we often must first check to see if we have "too many irons in the fire" keeping us from being able to fully commit.

One of a pastor's toughest jobs is trying to mobilize the congregation to participate in ministry. For a church to be vital and grow healthy disciples there must be a significant portion of the membership involved and serving in the ministries of the church.

It seems there is always a universal need for Sunday school and discipleship teachers, preschool, children and youth workers, greeters, worship team members, prayer warriors and the list goes on. All of these needs require commitment and sacrifice, causing many people to hesitate in getting involved. When a ministry opportunity is presented the main criteria is whether it conveniently fits into one's existing schedule. If the opportunity is the least bit uncomfortable then it is most likely a pass.

In Matthew we find the disciples out in the middle of the water in a boat being tossed around by high winds and giant waves. As far as the disciples knew, after Jesus sent them out in the boat to cross over to the other side of the lake, he then went somewhere to pray. Suddenly, out of the blackness of night comes a figure walking across the surface of the sea. I like Mark's account where it says He came to them walking on the sea and "would have passed them by."[31] Jesus wasn't afraid for their safety because he knew there was an accomplished seafaring man aboard the boat. He was simply going to meet them on the other side of the lake as promised. When they saw Jesus they assumed he was a ghost and cried out in fear. Jesus told them not to be afraid. "It's just me," he said.

Peter was excited about Jesus' mode of transportation and said, "Lord if it is you, let me come out there and walk on the water with you." Jesus said, "Come." Now this is the part of the story where everyone gets to rake Peter over the coals for not having enough faith. Peter stepped out of the boat and onto the water, but the moment he took his eyes off of Jesus he sank and cried out for Jesus to rescue him.

Peter's taking his eyes off of Jesus and crying out for help is a dominant message in this story. If the only golden faith nugget you take away from this story is how when Peter began to sink he reached out to Jesus for help you have missed what I believe is the most incredible fact of the story. Peter walked on the water! He was an experienced fisherman who understood how to navigate a boat through rough water. You can be sure this wasn't Peter's first storm at sea. When Jesus said, "Come," Peter left the safety and comfort of an environment he both knew well and trusted. He stepped overboard to walk on the water to Jesus!

Does Peter's bravery and willingness to even try to walk on water excite you as much as it does me? What would you have done? Most of us would have held on to the railing and said, "Well, I would. But jumping out of boats is just not my calling. It doesn't look too safe and success isn't guaranteed, so I'll just hang out here in the boat." Be honest, now. You know you most likely would not have just stepped over the rail and onto the water.

Another interesting thing to note in the story is Jesus did not call out to Peter by name. He looked toward the boat and said, "Come!" The invitation sounds wide open. It seems to me any of the men in the boat could have answered the call of Jesus' voice, yet only one ventured into the unknown to follow Christ.

Each week as I sit in church, I hear the voice of Christ say, "Come. The fields are ripe for harvest but I need more laborers." God needs people willing to step out of their boat and in faith walk to Him. You may get wet and may even sink a time or two, but just as Jesus was faithful to Peter he will be faithful to you. He did not let Peter drown and he will not let you drown. He will be with you with each step you take toward him. It may require you to throw out some of the scrap metal you call "irons in the fire," but there is more value in working for the Kingdom then there is in working for the temporal things of this world. Find a ministry, involve your whole family and train your kids to work alongside you in ministry. Venture outside the safe, warm and dry land of Benjamin. Sometimes the greatest adventures are experienced while hiking through the most challenging terrain.

The Land of Zuph

After Saul had passed through his homeland of Benjamin, he found himself in the land of Zuph. Zuph was probably named after Zuph the great-great-great-grandfather of Samuel, and was a district in which we find Samuel's city, Ramathaim-Zophim. The name "Zuph" means "honey" or "honeycomb."[32]

Personally, I have yet to meet anyone who does not like honey. Any time we use the word "honey" it is to denote something good to us. Often a cherished spouse is referred to as "Honey," or a good fishing spot can is called the "honey hole." Most of us get our honey the easy way, from the grocery store in a squeeze bottle shaped like a bear. Fresh honey is a little more difficult to obtain.

My father pastored a church in Ridgecrest, Louisiana for a number of years. There was a lady in our church named Sister Langston who owned a large house and rented out rooms as apartments. Three times a week I served as Sister Langston's taxi driver. Being that she did not drive she paid me to drive her to and from church.

One summer, Sister Langston discovered there were honey bees nesting in an entire wall of the old house structure. My dad and one of the deacons from the church rented beekeeper suits and equipment in order to remove the bees from her home. By the time my mom, brother, sister and I arrived on the scene in my 1978 AMC Gremlin the bee removal process had already begun. We exited the vehicle and immediately realized the bees were quite stirred up. We ran toward the house swatting and beating the air in an attempt to keep the aggravated bees from stinging us. Three out of the four of us were totally unsuccessful in our defense. My younger brother was seven years old at the time and didn't know any better than to calmly walk to the house without a swipe of his hand. In so doing, not one bee stung him. It was quite an experience for of all us. Yet, when the bees were completely removed and their nest disassembled, there was a large and sumptuous supply of honey for us all to divide. Of course, before we could enjoy it there was much filtering and purification necessary to get it ready for human consumption. It was delicious.

Honey is not always easy to find or obtain, but it *is* always sweet. Similarly, God's plan for our lives is rewarding and sweet. It isn't always easy to discover or simple to acquire, but it is always perfect for us and completely fulfilling.

Throughout this story we see a common thread; when Saul sought God, he discovered God's plan for his life. Matthew 6:33 says, "Seek first the Kingdom of God and His righteousness and all these things will be added to you." Additionally, David penned, "The steps of a righteous man are ordered by the Lord."[33] When we commit ourselves to seek God in the land of Zuph,

He will reveal to us His sweet purpose for our lives. Our steps will naturally be drawn to where He is leading us. Sometimes like Saul, on our mission to find what we think may be God's will for our lives we actually find God has something else in mind for us, something better. When we ask Him, He is always faithful to answer at just the right time. His best is always better than our best. If you are seeking to find God's will for your life, ask Him. He will show you in His time. Once you discover it, don't be afraid to step out of the boat. You must first step out of the boat if you want to walk on the water.

Chapter 5
Donkeys in the Desert

As I prepared for my Sunday school series on donkeys, my approach was to find every mention in the Bible of a donkey and then conduct an expository study. I discovered a donkey passage tucked away in Genesis but the mention was small and didn't seem too significant so I decided to move on in my search of the scriptures. As I tried to skip to the next donkey I felt compelled to look a little deeper.

The text says, "These were the sons of Zibeon: both Ajah and Anah. This was the Anah who found the water in the wilderness as he pastured the donkeys of his father Zibeon."[34] To get anything beneficial out of this story I needed to give it a closer look. I believe every word in God's inspired scripture is there for us to study, so there must be something worth knowing about this donkey reference.

In the beginning of Genesis chapter 36 we find the families of Jacob and Esau have grown too large to dwell in the same land and share the same resources. After discussing the options they made the decision to move apart. Esau, also called Edom, gathered his family and all of his possessions and moved to the land referred to as Mount Sier. When you see the "Edomites" referenced in the Bible, it is speaking of the family of Esau. As the chapter continues we see a list of the chiefs of the sons of Esau and then a separate list of the sons of Seir. Everyone gets a simple name mention except Anah. The text here is written using a familiar style making you think everyone knew Anah's story, as if you should respond, "Oh, that Anah!" After more than 5,000 years, the details of his story have been lost, but there still remain a few puzzle pieces we can fit together.[35]

Seir the Horite was the original inhabitant of the desolate mountainous area known by his name, Mount Seir. He actually has a known family tree. Seir was the son of Hur, who was the son if Hivi, the son of Canaan, son of Ham, who we know is the son of Noah. The term *horite* means cave dweller, and since this was a mountainous region we can deduce Seir and his family lived in caves. When Esau settled there it literally displaced the original inhabitants. Before Esau came on the scene, we are led to believe a heroic act was performed by Anah, the son of Zibeon.

A few facts about the identity of Anah are revealed in chapter 36. First, we see when Esau came to Mt. Seir, he married one of the daughters of Anah (Verses 2, 14 and 18). If you are a King James Version (KJV) enthusiast, there are a couple of things in this chapter which may be difficult to understand. In verses 2 and 14 it reads as if Anah is the daughter of Zibeon and then later says Anah is the son of Zibeon. This is because the original text has no word for granddaughter, so when it says "Aholibamah the daughter of Anah the daughter of Zibeon" (KJV), the meaning is Aholibamah is the daughter of Anah and the granddaughter of Zibeon. Most modern translations have improved this wording to portray the correct relationship.

The KJV has one other difference found in our verse 24, stating Anah found "mules" instead of "water" or, as some versions read, "hot springs." Scholars agree the interpretation as "mules" is based on a word which was corrupted and the meaning is certainly "water" or "hot springs."

Living in the Wilderness

When a new city is established, the first consideration is usually its proximity to a water source. If you think about major cities and communities in the United States, you will notice they settled there because the location was near a river, lake or some access to water. Water is an essential element for the livelihood of people, animals and crops. Without water we can't survive. Yet for some reason, Sier and his family settled in a dry, mountainous and desolate region located southwest of the Dead Sea. I'm sure Sier's father, Hur, was really proud of his son when he moved out and headed for the mountainous wasteland where there was not a drop of water to be found.

As I write this chapter, we are in the middle of one of the hottest, driest summers I have experienced in a long time. On occasion, there have been massive storm fronts rolling through our region, and when it nears our city it either falls apart or splits going both north and south of us and collides again on the other side. I have watched this phenomenon on the radar screen with amazement thinking, "How could this possibly happen? Is rain physically repelled from our city?" My grass and landscaping are on life support, and it is all I can do to keep them pumped with a little moisture.

It reminds me of a time as a child growing up in Ridgecrest, Louisiana. There was a prolonged period when we lacked rain. I remember the cracks in the ground opening wide enough to lose a G. I. Joe action figure somewhere in their depths. One day in particular, I thought it would be fun to run a water hose in one area of the yard and watch the cracks close up. Hours of hosing down the ground did little more than make the surface damp, and I never witnessed the cracks close even one centimeter.

We all know how important water is for our survival. For some reason, Sier decided to make a rocky desert a place to call home and raise his family. He had some sons, who had some sons, and Anah, the grandson of Seir, was to be the hero of the clan. He was responsible of taking care of his father's donkeys.

A donkey is quite suited to this dry type of environment, in fact more so than most domesticated animals. In such regions, donkeys were allowed to graze on the free range six to seven hours per day. They roamed some distances feeding on hay, shrubs and tree bark. Donkeys have a low water requirement, second only to the camel. Depending on the conditions, a donkey can consume from 18 to 35 liters of water per day. However, when there is a shortage of water they can live up to three days without a drop. They are also known to be very picky about the water they drink and will even turn down water they perceive as unclean.

Have you ever gone through a dry place in your life? Of course you have. We all have. Are you in one right now? We can find ourselves in a place where we are not growing spiritually, nothing seems to be happening and we aren't excited about the things of

God. I saw a cartoon years ago describing well exactly how these times feel.

In this one frame, there were two men on hands and knees crawling through the desert sands in stereotypical fashion with clothes tattered, dirty and sweaty. It was apparent they had wandered around for a long period of time. They look up and see a camel crawling on its belly, tongue hanging out and obviously in the same shape they were in. The camel was coming from the direction they were headed toward. One of the men looks at the other and says, "Well, this isn't a cheerful sign!"

In one frame, the cartoonist captured the hopelessness of how these times in our lives feel, like there is no end in sight. An endless drought drains the life out of everything. Some of you may be in the midst of what feels like an endless drought. This spiritual desert may be on a personal level, or it could even represent a phase a church body as a whole is living through. We find ourselves searching for satisfaction as we continue existing on dry grass and shrubs, going years with little water.

David related to these feelings in a Psalm he wrote when he was in the wilderness of Judah. "O God, You are my God; early will I seek You; my soul thirsts for You; my flesh longs for You in a dry and thirsty land Where there is no water."[36]

Our church was planning a drive-through "Living Nativity" for the Christmas season. It required a large cast, live animals and an elaborate set. We heard a nearby individual owned a camel. Camels aren't very common in South Arkansas, so it was worth checking into to see if we could rent the camel for our event. To our surprise, we learned the camel had died during the summer because it was too hot. Too hot for a camel... We're talking about a camel for crying out loud! Apparently, even camels have their limits and the Deep South proved to be more than it could bear. It is important for us to know how to survive during these hot, dry times in our lives so we don't meet the same fate as this unfortunate beast.

It is worthy to note that the two donkeys in the cast of animals were outstanding and survived quite well through the Arkansas summers. Perhaps camels are overrated as desert dwellers.

Facing the Drought

There are different ways people face these arid times in their spiritual walk. Some opt to retreat to a shady place of shelter, ration what little water they may have and stop exerting any unnecessary energy. They go into spiritual survival mode. The "survivor" will usually resign from responsibilities in the church or positions in ministry because they feel they have nothing to give, generally becoming uninvolved, unresponsive and isolated.

I can say this because I have experienced it first-hand. At the age of 19 I accepted a job as a youth pastor. I was so hungry to get involved I quickly donned a dozen hats. On top of youth ministry duties were bus driver, bulletin creator, worship leader, choir director, custodian as well as a few other job titles.

Over the course of the next 21 years I was involved in many avenues of ministry, including nine years on the road with my band Tinman Jones. At the end of my touring tenure I felt completely depleted of all energy as if I had little left to offer. For the next two years I avoided doing anything I could. I was content to sit in the pew and nothing else for the first time in my life. I was still a faithful church attender, I just didn't want to have to study, organize or practice for anything.

There are others who face these times of desiccation in a different manner altogether. There are the water chasers, who move from church to church and drive hundreds of miles to follow the next big revival or attend the next big "it" church. Don't get me wrong, there is nothing wrong with visiting an outpouring of the Spirit of God. But if the only way to stay hydrated in your Christian walk is to become a spiritual nomad, then the water you find will always be shallow. A spiritual drifter may succeed in getting a splash here and there, but they lack stability and the faithfulness God requires to be useful to the Kingdom of Heaven.

I believe God preserved this story in His living Word so we would be people like Anah, who discover water in the wilderness. Anyone can drink from a well dug by someone else. Knowing how to find water in the midst of your desert will not only keep you in supply of living water it will help you keep those around you in supply as well.

Anah found himself in a place where he could not go to someone else's land and water his donkeys. He was many miles from any known water source and his donkeys squeezed as much as they could out of the shrubs and cactus on which they fed.

One day, everything changed. It isn't recorded how water was found; whether Anah just wandered upon it or maybe the donkeys themselves found it. We don't know for sure but maybe he grew tired having no water and decided there must be water somewhere and found it through sheer determination. Whatever the method he used, he went down in the history of his region for his discovery and his actions are remembered to this day.

Finding Water in the Desert

When you find yourself in the desert of life, how do you find that much needed water source? We can draw some parallels to survival training. It is important to note there is always water to be found no matter how dry and desolate an area may seem. It may not be in the form of a geyser, or a beautiful lake, or even a flowing river, but there is water somewhere nearby. I believe the same is true in our lives. Even in your driest times when you feel your spirit crying out for a drop of life, Jesus is nearby with a drink of *living water* waiting to restore, refresh and redeem you.

Look For Signs of Life

There are three important survival methods we are going to explore in helping us find water in the desert. The first method to try when looking for water is to look for other signs of life; an animal, bird, mosquito, tree, even a blade of grass. Scan for an animal trail or tracks which may lead to a water source. All living creatures must have a certain amount of water to survive, so if you see anything living, they are getting water somewhere.

It is amazing to me to watch where some people go for advice. Jesus started a parable one time with, "Can the blind lead the blind? Will they not both fall into the ditch?"[82] I bet you can instantly name an incident of this phenomenon with someone you know. People have a tendency to talk to whom they are comfortable talking with rather than seeking someone likely to have the wisest answer. If you are going through a spiritual drought in your life and all the people you associate with are also in the same state, you will never find the refreshment you need. It may very well be if you are spending a lot of time with friends who resemble a spiritual Sahara, they may be the reason you are there in the first place. I know loyalty to friends can be a strong bond to break, but it might be time to look for friendships which show signs of life.

In John 5, Jesus met a man who was laid by a pool called Bethesda. This was a bath near what John referred to as "The Sheep Gate." The "Sheep Gate" is believed to be the gate by which the animals where brought in for sacrifice, and was located on the eastern wall of Jerusalem. The pool had five porches around it where many who were diseased, lame or otherwise sick would gather. Archaeological digs in the 19th century believe to have uncovered the location of a set of pools meeting the exact description for the Gospel's account, confirming their existence. There is a measure of debate about one portion of this story found in verse four, where an angel would come down at random times and "trouble" the water. When the water started to stir, the first one in would be healed of whatever disease they had.

The reason for the controversy is some translations concluded the text contained in verse four was added in later documents and was not in the original manuscripts. You can read this passage in various translations and see some include it and others do not. It is also believed by some this was a hot spring whose water would bubble up at irregular intervals because of gas accumulations in the rock caverns underneath the pool, and due to a lack of scientific knowledge of such things the belief of the angel troubling the water was an acceptable explanation. If indeed this was a hot spring, it would also give a clue as to why it would be considered a healing pool. Throughout time, many hot springs have been associated with healing properties, such as Hot Springs, Arkansas. If you are strict King James and insist on taking the part about the angel troubling the water literally, I will not argue with you. I only bring up the debate because it interested me as I explored this text.

The real story as it applies to this chapter is the fact this man had been laying beside this healing pool for 38 years. Nearly four decades is a long time to lay helpless, hoping something will happen. When Jesus asked him if he wanted to be made well the man explained he can't be made well because he had no one to help him to the water and he was not fast enough on his own to get there first. Are you getting the picture? He needed to get to the water, but everyone he was hanging around with were in the same condition he was; sick, lame and in bad health. No one among the company he kept was in any condition to help him. Why would they help him when it was their goal to get to the water first? If the man had friends who were well and capable of carrying him to the pool, then he may not have had to lay helpless for 38 years.

Bethesda means "House of Mercy." Yet there did not seem to be much mercy in the house until Jesus came along. He had to have an encounter with the giver of life. If you are in need of life, stop hanging around with the dead. They can't help you, they have nothing to give and their problems are too great for them to be able to see your needs.

Dig in Dry Streams or River Beds

The second method for finding water in the desert is to find what appears to be a dried up river or stream, maybe even a pond or lake bed. Even if it is cracked and crusty on top, there is a good chance there is still water at some level below the surface.

Dig a hole in one of these locations until you find damp ground, then keep digging until the water seeps forth. I learned in survival training you can dig a hole in the dried up river or lake, put a cup at the bottom center of the hole and lay a piece of plastic over the hole. Put a small rock on top of the plastic right in the center over the cup and let the plastic sink down to form a cone, then secure the plastic from sinking further into the hole. As the day heats up, moisture is drawn out of the ground. The plastic will prevent the water vapor from escaping into the air and allows it to condense on the underside of the plastic. Eventually, the water begins to run down the plastic toward the center and drips into the cup.

When trying to survive life's deserts it is easy to forget the times in our lives when we were spiritually refreshed and moving along with the flow of the living water. We look at our lives as a dry river bed or a drained lake and don't stop to think just below the surface we may find moisture.

After the death of Abraham, there was a famine in the land and Isaac took his family and moved away for a while. In his absence the Philistines moved in and stopped up all the wells of Abraham. This was a common tactic to fill your enemy's water well with sand. Isaac had prospered in the land where he had sought refuge from the famine and eventually the people asked him to leave because he had become too great among them. So he returned to the land God had promised Abraham to find all the wells had been filled with earth. Isaac's first order of business upon his return was to re-dig the wells which once flowed with clean and clear water.[37]

Digging for water in the spot of a previous well seems obvious, doesn't it? If a well once existed in a certain place then should water not still be down in that same location somewhere. Isaac thought so and he returned to the source which had been fruitful in the past. Many times we suffer because we stop doing the things we once did to keep the water flowing in our lives. We get busy and move on to other things and allow the enemy to slip in behind us and stop up the wells from which we once received our life giving source. Think back to a time in your life when you felt most in tune with God. A time when you felt blessed by His abundant presence. What were you doing then? Were you praying more? Reading your Bible more? Were there less commitments and obligations consuming your time? These are the things to look for when trying to identify what stopped up your well. Sometimes we need to return to the well where water once flowed in abundant supply and remove the sand clogging it up.

Aquariums are a lot of fun. I had a ten-gallon, fresh water aquarium for a while. Among the scores of fish which occupied my tank over time was a pair of fiddler crabs. These little crabs were especially entertaining. I like naming living creatures. I even have names for birds who frequently visit my yard. I named one of my fiddler crabs Toby.

I was sitting in my living room late one afternoon when all of a sudden I noticed something move across the room. I swung my head around to see what was scurrying across the floor. It was Toby! You can imagine my surprise when I spotted Toby out of the tank and scrambling across the floor. I scooped him up and promptly returned him to his home in the water.

A day or so later I found Toby out of the tank again. I was completely baffled as to how he was making his great escape. I went into detective mode staging a stakeout around the fish tank. The tank was nothing special. It had the typical blue rocks covering the floor, a cavernous structure for fish to take shelter, a plastic shrub in one corner and the water heater hanging down in the other corner.

As I watched from a discrete distance I saw Toby climb up into the shrub. He ascended to the top of the shrub and pushed off flapping his six little legs in frantic motion to keep himself from dropping to the rock bed below. Upon reaching the other corner, he lodged himself between the heater and the glass. Then with incremental pushing motions, he edged his way to the surface and climbed over the rim. His last act of bravery was dropping himself to the floor. Even though I was very impressed, I knew Toby would not survive long out of the tank so I returned him to the water. One day, not long after, I picked some clothing up off of the floor of the bedroom and there in its midst was Toby, dried up and lying lifelessly upside down with his legs curled.

Can you remember a time in your life when, like Toby, you found yourself feeling dried up and lying in the midst of a place you didn't belong? It is easy to allow activity, schedules, commitments or maybe the mundane things of everyday life to lure us away from the life-sustaining water and into a time of drought and despair.

Our desire to wander can lead to a spiritual thirst we can only quench by returning to the water of life. The Lord asked John while on the Isle of Patmos to write a letter to the church at Ephesus. In his letter he began by praising the great works they were doing, then pointed out in the midst of doing great works they had left their first love. They were instructed to return to their first love, to the "first works," the things they once held dear. The word "repent" was used, which sounds strong considering they were doing all manner of great works. Repent means to "turn around." Even our good intentions and great works can bring us to a dry place. When we find ourselves in a parched condition, we must turn around and re-dig the wells. Once the water is again flowing into your well, lower your bucket and fetch a refreshing drink.

Welcome the Storms

Even in the driest desert, there is an occasional storm. If you are stranded without water, the coming deluge is a welcome sight. Find any type of container you can and collect as much of the rain water as possible.

You may recall Hurricane Charlie which entered the Gulf of Mexico in 2003 and made a hard hook before hitting the West Coast of Florida. Charlie continued to wreak havoc as he forged across the state and exited the eastern beaches into the Atlantic. He picked up steam once he re-entered the warm ocean waters, hooked left and headed back inland toward Myrtle Beach, South Carolina.

It just so happened, Tinman Jones was scheduled to perform at a college in Myrtle Beach. We arrived earlier in the day to set the stage for the show slated to start promptly at seven that evening. We received word Myrtle Beach was under a mandatory evacuation order starting at six o'clock, just one hour prior to our scheduled concert. We decided the show must go on, so we continued as planned for the 25 or so people who were still in town.

At the conclusion of the show, we quickly broke down the equipment, packed the trailer and pointed the nose of the bus west. The line of traffic was the worst I had ever seen as the population streamed out of harm's way. I had the privilege of driving the first shift and it took us literally four hours to travel the first 30 miles. The bus was gasping for diesel fumes, and even with a truck stop within site it took an unimaginable amount of time to navigate the bumper-to-bumper sea of automobiles all attempting to outrun the storm. We refueled just in time and made it to a North Carolina parking lot where we rode out the remnants of the storm.

When drawing analogies to life, storms almost always represent something bad, a difficult circumstance or a troubling time. Storms are thought to be destructive and draining. We do whatever we can to avoid the storms of life and pray Jesus famous words, "Peace be still." Storms can be destructive, yet they also bring refreshing rain.

Even though it may seem people today are more selfish than ever, isolated and oblivious to needs around them, it still amazes me to see people rally around their neighbors when trouble strikes. When a storm hits, there are many in churches, work places or the community who move to give aid with prayers, donations and all manner of support. I'm not advocating praying for storms so people will feel sorry for you and help you to a better place. I'm just suggesting you do not have to be afraid of the storm.

It seems when trouble comes he often brings all of his buddies with him. You may feel alone while in the midst of a dry season when all of sudden the tempest comes blowing in. It is easy to feel a sense of panic when storms come at a low point in your life. However, it may be a vehicle of salvation God is orchestrating from which to deliver you or perhaps He's bringing rescue to many.

Some friends of mine are a stunning example of how to weather a storm and use it to bring living water to thousands of others in need. Chaney and Jessica Phillips were living in South Texas when they felt God's call on their lives. They sold everything and moved to New Orleans with their two daughters to undergo a season of training. They had not been there long when their three-year-old, Brooke, became ill. A series of tests revealed their beloved child had leukemia.

Living directly in the path of Hurricane Katrina they evacuated from New Orleans to Houston, Texas. There Brooke received cancer treatment at Texas Children's Hospital. It is reasonable to think many questions must have filled their minds during this time. I'm sure they asked, "Why us when we were giving all to follow You?" Even though they were persons of incredible faith they were definitely in the midst of a storm while walking through a desert.

Brooke became their shining ray of hope during this overcast and cloudy season of their lives. Brooke had an incredible gift to love. One day as they were sitting together in Brooke's room in Children's Hospital, they heard a child crying out in pain in the next room. Though Brooke was suffering herself and hooked up to all manner of devices, she grabbed her dad by the hand and said, "We need to pray for that baby!" She constantly blew kisses and made "I Love You" gestures with her hand to everyone who entered or exited her room. The truth is she lifted the spirits of those who thought they were coming to lift hers.

She fought bravely through chemotherapy, bone marrow transplant and treatments for two years. Then, on September 29, 2006, Brooke went to be with Jesus. Instead of becoming bitter and blaming God for sending the storm, the Phillip's gathered the containers of water from the storm and started an organization today known as B.I.G. (Brook's Incredible Gift) Love Cancer Care. The Phillip's family is passionately reaching out and providing care to families of children with cancer in both Arkansas Children's Hospital and Texas Children's Hospital, two facilities where Brooke received treatment. They have amassed an army of volunteers who pass out toys, necessary items and even provide housing to these families in need. Not only did they find water in their desert, but they are now giving water to thousands.

Take Action to Find Water

Every time we face the deserts of life action is required on our part if we want to get through them. It required effort to seek out life, re-dig the wells and stand in the storm holding a bucket. Moses led over a million thirsty people through the wilderness. One time he struck a rock and water came out. Another time he had to cut a tree down into a pool to purify it. On another occasion he disobeyed and struck a rock when he was told to speak to the rock, yet water still flowed to the people.

In each of the cases action was required. In your personal desert you will need to shake off the urge to crawl into a shady crag and merely hope for a way out. You have to take action in order to find water for your soul. Refreshment and restoration will come when you allow the ever-flowing river of living water to renew your soul.

Jesus says in the book of John, "If anyone thirsts, let him come to Me and drink. He who believes in Me, as the Scripture has said, out of his heart will flow rivers of living water."[38] Jesus keeps a supply of living water within all of us. Sometimes it takes some digging, purification or a willingness to unclog some pipes in order to get it flowing again. It is God's desire for you to be a wellspring of life with his water flowing out of you.

The name "Anah" in Hebrew means "be humbled." Anah was just Zibeon's son, the donkey herder, who spent his entire days in the desert with a bunch of sweaty and stinky donkeys. His hard work wasn't glamorous or exciting and often went unnoticed. There is another mention of Anah in the book of Genesis where the same man is referred to by the name of

"Beeri." When I found out what the name "Beeri" translated to, it floored me; "Beeri" means "the well" or "man of the wells."[39] He came to the desert as Anah, the humbled donkey herder. After Anah discovered water in the desert which brought much needed life to the entire region he became known as "the man of the wells" or simply The Well! My prayer is, "Lord, make me a man of the wells." You, too, can join me in this prayer so the dry climate does not destroy you but makes you a conduit of living water to the world around you.

Maybe you are in the middle of a desert, a dry place in your life where you and your donkeys are wandering day after day with little refreshment. Don't just sit down in the shade and hope for a better day. Search out the blessings of God, find the living water and allow it to spring forth from within you. Be a wellspring of life to your world. The water is there, even in the desert. Be willing to take action and find it.

Chapter 6
Counting Donkeys

W hy is it when we are having trouble falling to sleep we are told to count sheep? I've never actually tried the sheep counting method myself. It seems seeing sheep jump over a fence against a backdrop of an endless green meadow would be too distracting to propel me into a restful slumber. The truth is if I want to go to sleep fast all I need to do is pick up a book. After just one page of reading you will hear me snoring. Maybe polling sheep actually works for some. If we assume counting livestock among the remedies for healing sleeplessness, than I propose a method for keeping anger in check...counting donkeys! Six to be exact. Let me explain.

In 1 Samuel we find David has been anointed as the next king and King Saul does not like it one bit. You see, Saul was on the hunt for David, and David was in hiding. David had amassed a group of about 600 men all living in the Wilderness of Paran located in the southern regions of Israel and rich in Biblical history. When Hagar left Abraham and Sarah with her son, Ishmael, the Wilderness of Paran became their home.

It was this wilderness area where the Children of Israel set down camp when the spies were sent into Canaan.[40] It was also on this desolate property with its gravel-laced plateau, red canyons and occasional acacia tree adorning the landscape David found refuge. Shepherds brought their flocks of sheep to these fields to roam under careful watch. David, a former shepherd turned warrior, relating to these herdsmen offered them voluntary protection against predatory wildlife and outlaws who poached sheep and on occasion mugged travelers. David's men always acted honorably when performing these defensive duties and never harassed the shepherds nor stole from them. In return, they received provisions from the businessmen who owned the flocks.

Among these businessmen there was a wealthy man named Nabal who worked in wool trade and had over 6,000 sheep and goats. The text refers to him as very harsh and shrewd in his financial dealings. Ironically, the name "Nabal" means "fool." Nabal had a lovely wife, Abigail, who was described as "a woman of good understanding and beautiful appearance."[41]

A great celebratory event is taking place at this point in the story...shearing day. It is a day filled with many feasts and parties and brimming with a carnival-like spirit in the air. David sent ten servants to Nabal to ask for the customary provisions expected for their protection services. This kept Nabal's losses to a minimum and his profits up. Nabal refused to offer any tribute and sent the men away empty-handed with their ears filled with harsh words. David took great offense at this; similar to how you might feel if after putting in a forty-hour work week your boss yelled at you for expecting your paycheck and sent you home empty-handed.

There is, however, another way to look at this scenario. David's "voluntary" service in which payment in return was expected sounds similar to a guy who jumps out at a red light and without being asked to do so proceeds to wash your car windows and then expects to be tipped for his efforts.

On one trip with the band, as we were leaving a concert in Ft. Worth, Texas, we discovered we were in desperate need of fuel. We weren't sure we could make it to the nearest truck stop where we usually fueled our bus. When you are filling a 140-gallon tank you really want the big hose. With the needle pushing too close to "E" we decided to find diesel anywhere we could, so we stopped at an ordinary gas station close to the interstate. As the fuel streamed slowly through the tiny hose we settled in for a bit of a break. Without warning, a man jumped on the front bumper of the bus with a squeegee and began washing our windows. It felt like an invasion, a little violating, and we knew we were in for a shake-down. A couple of us politely asked him to back away, explaining we did not wish to have this service performed. Fortunately for us, he did not smash the windshield out of spite. We stopped the fueling and headed out toward the Interstate as quickly as we could.

Perhaps Nabal felt like he was being taken advantage of, or extorted. Whether David was justified or not, a vengeful spirit erupted and he ordered 400 of his men to don their armor and weapons with full intent to kill Nabal, his servants and anyone who got in the way. One of Nabal's servants found Abigail and told her the details of the day and how David was on his way to make an example of Nabal. Abigail quickly loaded a train of donkeys with provisions to take to David for the purpose of persuading him to extend mercy.

Why I Oughtta…

It is always funny to me to see an old movie and hear the phrase, "Why I oughtta!" The proclaimer of the threat while waving a fist around never reveals what it is he is going to do, but he sounds extremely intent about accomplishing his mission. We all have our "Why I oughtta" moments. My mom's favorite retaliatory line was, "I'm going to write them a letter!" Any time she was wronged, or one of her family or friends was a victim of commercial mistreatment, she would threaten to launch a hand-written postal assault. I can just envision the executive of a company sitting in his high-back executive chair behind his big oak desk in his plush high-rise office when a courier comes in waving "the letter!" He shrinks beneath the desk with a fading, "Noooooooooooooo! Not the letter!"

Once, my wife Terri actually did write *the letter*. She had purchased a bicycle inner tube from a national retail chain and once home discovered the box had been cut all the way through the inside tube rendering it useless. When she returned the item she was told it had been returned before and inadvertently placed back on the shelf for resale. They allowed the exchange. She submitted the experience on an online feedback service and later received a response from a manager explaining someone had been fired over the incident. She felt terrible as she never intended to cause someone to lose their job. I learned you never want Terri writing *the letter*, it carries a lot of weight!

We are a people who demand justice. "How dare they do that to me!" is a recurring theme in today's society. When I was a kid, we joked about the passage in the Bible, "Turn the other cheek," pointing out it doesn't say what to do after you have turned the other cheek. Once the second cheek is struck, it was time to fight back. In the natural we all feel justified in taking revenge. It isn't just people with whom we get crossways. I have been known to exact vengeance on inanimate objects when something I am working on isn't cooperating. I want to kick it, or throw it, shake it, or just let out a gruff, "Come on!" Although my display of aggression toward objects has lessened as I realize if I throw something I have to retrieve it, or worse, if I break it I have the added aggravation and expense of replacing it.

David reacted quickly by calling his men to arms without analyzing the situation or stopping to count the long-term effects of his actions. David was anointed as the next King of Israel and would eventually be King over Nabal and this whole area. Did he ever stop to think how his actions would affect his ability to rule these people? Did he think about what his actions would do to his reputation? No, his thoughts were focused on his immediate emotion and how to administer swift justice in order to save his ego from suffering a blow.

Our actions and reactions as Christians have wider implications than our immediate situation or the things going on in our personal worlds. I have tried to witness to people who would not accept what I was saying because someone in their past who claimed to be a Christian had wronged them. It is true that some people will use anything as an excuse to reject your message, and unfortunately they are being lied to by the devil to keep them separated from God. There are also traces of truth to their grievance.

I have a friend who works in a billing office and occasionally receives calls from "church people" who are rude and demanding. Most of the time they are unaware they are speaking to someone who knows them personally. My friend's faith is unshakable, but what about those who may be sitting on the fence of faith and receive call after call like this. Is this the picture of Christianity we should be painting for the world? When we let anger dictate our actions we not only damage our own witness, but we also damage the witness of others. I totally understand the sentiment though, believe me! I remember getting so frustrated while talking with a long distance carrier about my service I literally yelled in the phone and slammed the receiver down repeatedly no less than half a dozen times. I look back on my display with no great pride.

Hey, we are talking about human nature here, to which we all fall victim. Another term for "human nature" is "flesh," something in which we are supposed to find a way to crucify and not live in accordance to. How do we squelch the need to lash out at others in rage by giving someone a piece of our mind when honestly we really don't have much of our mind to spare in the first place? Abigail brought a caravan of donkeys and in so doing she calmed David's wrath. What do you think it was about these donkeys that made David relent? Perhaps, had Abigil ridden out alone to plead with David, he would have dismissed her and continued with his unabated plan. The offering she brought packed atop a donkey train made David stop and consider what he was doing.

The Donkey of Bread

Abigail loaded 200 loaves of bread onto the first donkey. Who in the world has 200 loaves of bread just sitting around? That's a lot of dough! It is possible the loaves of bread had been prepared for the feast day and Abigail just redirected them for a different purpose. I believe the number of loaves is significant and completely applicable to us today.

200 is often referred to as a number of insufficiency in the Bible. Achan took 200 shekels of silver from Jericho yet it was not sufficient to save him from his sin of disobedience.[42] Absalom's hair weighing 200 shekels did not save him from the tree.[43] For 200 sheckels, Micah bought a graven image which led Israel into idolatry and revealed the insufficiency of religion.[44] In John 6:8 we hear Phillip say, "200 denarii worth of bread is not sufficient" to feed the multitude.

Repeatedly, we are reminded the number 200 is not enough, so what bridges the gap between insufficient and completion? Jesus took a measly two loaves of bread and increased the small offering making it sufficient to feed 5,000 plus people! He explained in John 6:35, "I am the bread of life. He who comes to me shall never hunger, and he who believes in me shall never thirst.'" This Bread was broken revealing His grace is sufficient for us.[45] In our state of insufficiency, Christ extended his grace to us so we can be made sufficient, whole and acceptable before God; a reminder of the grace in which Jesus measures us and in turn this should give us a desire to show grace to others.

I had seven shirts and three pair of pants at the cleaners ready to be picked up. This particular cleaners didn't give out tickets or receipts when you dropped off your clothes, you just gave them your name and out the door you went. When I arrived to pick up my cleaned clothing, I gave them my name; however, they could not locate any of my garments. Fortunately, they gave me the benefit of the doubt and a massive search ensued.

A few short minutes passed before they shut down all other operations and asked every available employee to search for my clothing. The conveyers were spinning and a parade of thin plastic sheathed groupings of shirts was passed to me for inspection. Over and over the manager offered his apologies. Near 30 minutes passed when suddenly, like a ray of light beaming from the crowded rack, my clothes appeared nicely pressed and ready for wear.

I was relieved the wait was over, but was surprised at my ability to stay calm through the entire fiasco. I realized God had given me an extra measure of grace, which compelled me not to make a big deal about a frustrating circumstance. Instead of reacting negatively I repeatedly assured the manager, "It's okay. No problem. After all, they are just shirts and pants."

How embarrassing for me it could have been had I stomped around and thrown a big tirade only to have one of those employees visit my church the next Sunday and see me playing bass on the worship team while lifting my hands and praising God. This reaction certainly would have left them thinking, "Yeah, we know what you are really like!"

I think all of us in our daily lives sometimes forget we are dealing with humans. Too often we view the world like a well-oiled machine expecting everyone and everything to perform flawlessly and without a hitch. We forget the fact we are interacting with people just like us who have been given the same gift of grace by Jesus Christ we too received. Jesus said it best when he queried the group of accusers with, "He that is without sin among you, let him first cast a stone."[46]

Viewing The Donkey of Bread reminds us of the *bread of life* who came to cover our shortcomings and sin with his all sufficient grace. We all fall short of the glory of God and yet God's grace looks beyond our faults and in the same way we should look beyond the faults of others with this same grace we are so freely given.

The Donkey of Wine

Most translations describe the second donkey as carrying two skins of wine, although a few translations substitute the word "bottles" or "jugs." In any case, the application is not referring to a small quantity. A "skin of wine" refers to the practice of taking the hide from a goat without tearing; then sewing, or sealing the end of the legs, neck, or other openings and using it as a container. In today's parallel, it is like saying two kegs of wine, which make it proportional to the rest of the provisions of the offering.

Wine is often used when speaking of the Holy Spirit. Ephesians 5:18 says, "Do not be drunk with wine, but be filled with the Spirit." On The Day of Pentecost a reference is made to the 120 who were drunk with new wine when they had received the initial infilling of the Holy Spirit.

Generally, wine is made from fermented fruit which is a process often compared to the ongoing work of the Holy Spirit within the heart of man. In Galatians we find a list of what is known as the fruits of the Spirit. These are attributes we should walk out through our actions, which reflect the Spirit of God working in our lives.[47]

Growing up, my family lived in the church parsonage while my dad pastored in Ridgecrest, Louisiana. This quarter-acre property had an amazing assortment of fruit trees; some plum trees, a pair tree, peach tree, a couple of apple trees, a very large fig tree, a pecan tree and a catalpa tree. All the trees grew lots of healthy fruit. It was great as a kid, to walk out into the backyard and pluck a juicy peach or plum right off the tree and enjoy eating it on the spot.

I told my Bible study class this story and asked them if they knew what kind of fruit the Catalpa tree produced. Funny, almost every one of them responded with, "a worm," although the moment it left their mouth you could tell it didn't quite sound right. Of course everyone knows, a tree can't produce a worm as its fruit. The fruit of a Catalpa tree is a long, thin purple bean! You see, the tree is not known for its fruit, but rather a worm which is attracted to the tree. Many a fisherman has found the Catalpa worm, as it is called, useful for fishing. However, in a broader sense, it is quite the pest eating the leaves of the tree and leaving behind a path of destruction. These Catalpa worms come during a specific season and cover the tree as well as the ground around it. They make such an impression the tree is known for this worm rather than its fruit.

Did you know, "We are known by our fruit?"[48] By showing love, joy, peace and the other peaches and plums on the list, we not only gain a reputation of producing good fruit, we also give the world a good taste of Christ and his love for them. What type of fruit do others see manifested through your life? Given the choice, what kind of tree do you want to be, a fruit-bearing tree or one known as a worm tree?

The Donkey of Sheep

Abigail loaded donkey number three with five dressed sheep. In Palestine, sheep had many purposes; their wool was desired for clothing, some were used as a sacrifice, as well as other things. The five sheep presented to David could not be used for sacrificial purposes because they had been dressed and therefore were deemed unfit. Neither could they be used for clothing as they had no wool to shear. Given their condition, the only purpose for which these sheep were suitable was for their meat. I'm not sure how far the meat of five sheep would go in feeding a mob of 600 hungry soldiers. However, one thing is for sure, David's band of mighty men was not the type to live on bread alone. I can relate, as I am a steak and potato kind of guy. I will occasionally play with a salad, but bring on the meat! I don't eat "cheese pizza" and prefer a side of sausage with my pancake stack.

In Hebrews, Paul talks straight with the church admonishing them to be teachers and leaders. He is frustrated, as they are still wanting to be spoon fed the basic principles of God (the milk) rather than choosing to grow in their maturity and be fed the greater disciplines (the meat) of God.[49] Meat or "solid food" as it translates in modern versions represents spiritual maturity. I find it entertaining to watch the ways people behave around babies, and who can blame them; they are cute. That is at least most of them. They represent innocence, and even when they act out at times, their behavior is always excused by the phrase, "They just don't know any better." The more the child matures, the less we tolerate certain behaviors as we recognize they should know better how to control their actions.

No one likes to be told, "Grow up!" That is exactly what Paul was telling the church in this letter, to move beyond childish things and take a more mature role as a follower of Christ. Paul's instruction is totally applicable in this context. As children mature, they grow through different phases of possessiveness, defensiveness and selfishness. With maturity they learn the value in principles like sharing, getting along well with others and not always insisting on their own way. As Christians, growth is marked by developing traits such as forgiveness, kindness, loving your neighbor as yourself and going the extra mile. These are all signs of spiritual maturity.

I don't know anyone who doesn't like an occasional episode of "America's Funniest Home Videos." There is one clip I recall where a toddler was throwing a massive tantrum while sprawled on the floor crying in protest over who knows what. The family member holding the camera backed away from the scene and moved out of sight into an adjacent room. Almost immediately, the room grew quiet. With the camera aimed at the doorway, the kid emerged into view and threw himself on the floor continuing the tantrum. Again, the camera person backed away from the scene and into another room and within seconds the wailing ended. Just as before, the little fellow trotted around the corner, and once in view fell to the floor continuing the fit. Such a scene is hilarious when the subject is two years old, but it is a lot less laughable when the child is a 35-year-old father of three throwing a tantrum.

Aren't we doing exactly the same thing when we throw a visible display of displeasure over something which really doesn't matter much when compared with the realm of eternity? Vengeance and retaliation aren't often reactions carried out in secret. They are typically displayed publically in hopes of making the statement one has evened the score. Such a display may give temporary personal satisfaction, yet it really only demonstrates a total lack of maturity.

The third donkey's purpose is to remind us to "Grow up" and eat the meat of God's word. As mature Christians we must leave the milk for the babies, those new to the faith.

The Donkey of Roasted Grain

The next donkey on parade was loaded with five seahs of roasted grain. In researching exactly how much a "seah" represents in dry measure, I found there is no small disagreement as to what this measure translates. Some versions define seah as one bushel while others define it as two bushels. I did find some resources define seah as one-third of an ephah if this helps you any. To draw an obscure conclusion let's say it was between one and two bushels of roasted grain.

Grain was one of the biggest staples at this time and wheat and barley were the two main types of grain primarily grown and traded. The most primitive way to eat grain was right out of the field and the more sophisticated was to eat it roasted. Since Abigail brought roasted grain it was most likely threshed.

Threshed grain was more valuable than grain containing all the freshly harvested chaff and husks.

There are many references to the separation of the chaff from the wheat in both the Old and New Testaments. Once the grain was threshed by beating it with broom-like tools, it was tossed into the air allowing the wind to blow the lighter husk aside, leaving the grain to fall alone. This chafing and threshing represents the same type of separation we as Christians should have from the world. As we allow the wind of the Holy Spirit to blow into our lives and remove the attitudes and impulses of the flesh, we should be left with the purity of the fruit of the Spirit.

We can draw another parallel from observing this donkey of grain. In the book of John, Jesus explains it this way, "Most assuredly, I say to you, unless a grain of wheat falls into the ground and dies, it remains alone; but if it dies, it produces much grain. He who loves his life will lose it, and he who hates his life in the world will keep it for eternal life."[50]

When someone commits an offense against you, it is completely natural, in the flesh, to desire to repay wrong for wrong. It requires a deliberate act of choice to hold back and deny the human will from seeking revenge. By dying to yourself, you allow more of Christ to live through you. When we die to our natural desires, just as the grain dies when it falls to the ground, God multiplies his good through us and by his grace the lives of others are changed as well.

The Donkey of Raisins

The fifth donkey carried 100 clusters of raisins. Raisins were a common staple given to someone on a long journey. David had a long, physical journey ahead of him. It required he look beyond his immediate circumstances and toward the path lying ahead.

Reacting irrationally to a situation is also known as being short-sighted. It is when we choose to do what brings momentary satisfaction rather than thinking through the negative consequences such actions bring to relationships, our testimony, our reputation or even future opportunities. Raisins are here to remind us to prepare ourselves for the long journey ahead.

Post-college I worked for a short time at a convenience store. If you have worked at such a place you will understand what I mean when I say it was an interesting experience all the way around. I saw many of the same people every day, some stopped by to purchase a newspaper, others bought their daily allotment of cigarettes, others just wanted a cold drink...you get the picture.

There was this one little old lady who would come in every day at about the same time and buy two dollars of gas. I am sure you are smiling right about now, but this was the mid-eighties when a dollar went a little farther at the pump. Each day she put two dollars' worth of fuel into her old brown Ford Maverick. She paid with two moist bills pulled from an unmentionable location laying them carefully on the counter. I discretely picked up the soggy bills by their corners and put them gingerly into the register. I often wondered why she didn't just purchase ten dollars of gas once per week. This little old lady must have lived literally on a day-to-day budget.

The Bible teaches us not to worry about tomorrow, and yet we need not live as if there is no tomorrow. Our life is a long journey, and the seeds we sow today do grow and produce a harvest at a later date. We must take note of the raisins in our life and be careful not to live so in-the-moment we later have regrets.

The Donkey of Figs

The final donkey was packed with 200 cakes of figs. Figs are one of the most commonly named fruits in the Bible. In fact, the first tree mentioned in Genesis is a fig tree. We see it mentioned when Adam and Eve sewed fig leaves together to hide their nakedness in the Garden of Eden. Figs are also a symbol of peace. We find a reference in 1 Kings 4:25 about life in Israel under the reign of King Solomon. God had blessed Solomon with peace on every side and everyone "dwelt safely, each man under his vine and his fig tree."

Among the Fruits of the Spirit listed in Galatians, peace is third on the list behind love and joy, therefore it must be pretty important to make the top three. In Matthew, Jesus had an encounter with a fig tree. He returned to the city hungry and spotted a fig tree by the road. He approached the tree to find nothing but leaves and declared the tree would never again produce fruit. The tree withered away by the next day.[51] Perhaps this can be applied to a life not bearing the fruit of peace. When our words and actions lead to conflict and retribution how can we be a person who produces spiritual fruit?

One thing is for certain; acting angrily in a situation seldom renders the desired result but rather stirs up more ire. We find this principle illustrated perfectly in the scripture, "A soft answer turns away wrath, but a harsh word stirs up anger."[52] There is no guarantee a soft response will defuse every volatile situation. There will always be belligerent people who, no matter what you do, will choose to be difficult. I agree with Paul when he says, "If it is possible, as much as depends on you, live peaceably with all men."[53] It often doesn't only depend solely on us. We can't control the actions of others but we can control our own actions by choosing to be men and women of peace. I believe God greatly honors our attempts to live peacefully. When you think of the last donkey carrying the figs may it remind you of the big picture and may you be encouraged to choose the peaceful solution.

Be Angry, But Do Not Sin

"Be angry, but do not sin. Do not let the sun go down on your wrath, nor give place to the devil."[54] Often we cannot help the emotions within us that rise-up when we are wronged or when faced with an injustice. It is our responsibility to respond in a manner which will not be sinful through growing in God's disciplines.

After Abigail captured David's attention with the parade of loaded donkeys, she spoke inspiring words which turned David's heart of revenge away from its present course of destruction.

"So she fell at his feet and said: "On me, my lord, on me let this iniquity be! And please let your maidservant speak in your ears, and hear the words of your maidservant. Please, let not my lord regard this scoundrel Nabal. For as his name is, so is he: Nabal is his name, and folly is with him! But I, your maidservant, did not see the young men of my lord whom you sent. Now therefore, my lord, as the LORD lives and as your soul lives, since the LORD has held you back from coming to bloodshed and from avenging yourself with your own hand, now then, let your enemies and those who seek harm for my lord be as Nabal. And now this present which your maidservant has brought to my lord, let it be given to the young men who follow my lord. Please forgive the trespass of your maidservant. For the LORD will certainly make for my lord an enduring house, because my lord fights the battles of the LORD, and evil is not found in you throughout your days. Yet a man has risen to pursue you and seek your life, but the life of my lord shall be bound in the bundle of the living with the LORD your God; and the lives of your enemies He shall sling out, as from the pocket of a sling. And it shall come to pass, when the LORD has done for my lord according to all the good that He has spoken concerning you, and has appointed you ruler over Israel, that this will be no grief to you, nor offense of heart to my lord, either that you have shed blood without cause, or that my lord has avenged himself."[55]

David listened to her and realized there were still many angles he had not considered in calling his men to arms. He thanked Abigail for her intervention and advice.

Paul gives us words of wisdom in his letter to the Romans when he says, "Repay no one evil for evil. Have regard for good things in the sight of all men. If it is possible, as much as depends on you, live peaceably with all men. Beloved, do not avenge yourselves, but rather give place to wrath; for it is written, 'Vengeance is Mine, I will repay,' says the Lord. Therefore If your enemy is hungry, feed him; If he is thirsty, give him a drink; For in so doing you will heap coals of fire on his head. Do not be overcome by evil, but overcome evil with good."[56] Responding in love to others who have hurt you is not always easy, but it is always the right thing to do. The Lord reserves the right to administer justice. In Nabal's case, justice was served the same night he had a heart attack and died. David heard of this and sent for Abigail to be his wife.

Don't make a way for anger to take up residence in your life. Let the principles of these donkeys guide you to a better resolution and choose to live pursuing peace.

Chapter 7
Jawbone Moments

The story of our next donkey is one with which we are all too familiar. In the book of Judges we find Israel has fallen again into wickedness and sinned in the sight of the Lord. What else is new, right? These people have more ups and downs than a Classic Duncan at a Yo-Yo convention. This time it won them 40 years in the hands of the Philistines. As usual the people would cry out to God and repent, and God devised a plan to deliver His people from the enemy. An angel appeared to Mr. Manoah and Mrs. Zorah announcing they would have a son. This lad would be set apart from birth to take the Nazarite vow. The Nazarite vow, in most instances, was voluntary. It was taken by any man or woman who desired to separate themselves to the Lord for a season. The apostle Paul took this vow for the 18 months he was in the wretched city of Corinth. Paul's hair cut upon leaving Corinth gives us a clue.[57] To learn more about the specifics of the Nazarite vow read Numbers 6:1–8.

Following Samson's birth he didn't get the privilege of choosing whether or not to take this vow, it was his burden to bear from day one. He grew up and physically became a very strong young man.

One day he returned home from town and told his dad, "I found a woman I like among the daughters of the Philistines. Go get her for me!" Mom and Dad, in an effort to talk him out of this decision, questioned why he couldn't find a local girl. Samson insisted saying, "For she pleases me very well!" If you are the parent of a teenager a conversation such as this may have a familiar ring. Samson did not listen to the voice of reason, so the deal was made and the marriage arranged.

Next, Samson went to Timnah, the city where his new bride-to-be lived. On his way there, a young lion charged him. Samson, his strength so great, tore the lion in two with his bare hands. Later, on his trip back home he turned aside to see the carcass, and to his surprise, bees had already turned the dead lion into a hive filled with honey. Samson reached into the lion and drew out some honey. He ate some and took the rest home, giving it to his mom and dad. However, he did not disclose from where the honey had come.

At a wedding, Samson posed a riddle to 30 young men attending the feast, "Out of the eater came something to eat, and out of the strong came something sweet." The men, unable to solve the riddle, begged Samson's new wife to find out for them.

Samson's wife convinced him to give her the answer which she willingly shared. The 30 young men returned to Samson giving him the correct answer to the riddle...a lion. Samson aware of what had happened replied, "If you had not plowed with my heifer, you would not have solved my riddle!" We could never get away with such a statement these days.

Samson killed 30 Philistines that day taking their clothes as payment for his bet. His father-in-law responded by giving his daughter's hand in marriage to the best man. The conflict continued to escalate until the Philistines threatened all of Israel if they did not turn Samson over to them.

They sent 1,000 soldiers to capture Samson and he allowed himself to be bound by ropes and delivered to the Philistine army. On the trip back, Samson snapped those ropes, found the skeleton jawbone of a donkey and used it to slaughter the entire army. I think Samson was even surprised by his great victory due to the help of such an unlikely weapon because he named the place Ramath Lehi, which meant "Jawbone Height."

Thank you for patiently reading through my rendition of a story you may have previously heard a million times. I have listened to no small number of sermons myself on every angle of this story except one. What about the donkey? Sure, Samson only wielded a donkey jawbone, but the jawbone once belonged to a living, breathing, grey-coated beast of burden.

What do we know about this donkey? Absolutely nothing! To me the lack of information makes the story all the more interesting. During the donkey's living years I imagine it carried riders and cargo, and experienced many things over its 30 to 50 years of life. It probably had owners who loved and took great care of it. Remember, donkeys were a valuable and cherished asset. Over the span of this donkey's life, not one single memory was recorded, yet nearly 4,000 years later there is still one thing about which stories are told. Its jawbone was the weapon God provided for Samson to use in delivering the Children of Israel.

This great victory gave the Children of Israel 20 years of peace apart from the oppression of the Philistines. The biggest impact of this donkey's life was made after its death. It was what he left behind which made a lasting difference.

Jawbone Moments

The theme this donkey brings to the story is a question; "What do we leave behind?" The Apostle Paul encourages us "...since we are surrounded by so great a cloud of witnesses, let us lay aside every weight, and the sin which so easily ensnares us, and let us run with endurance the race set before us."[58] I've heard some strange teaching on just whom this "cloud of witnesses" is referring. However, when you read the previous chapter you realize it refers to the many heroes of the faith.

Abel offered a better sacrifice. Enoch pleased God so much he did not have to experience death. Noah became an instrument of the preservation of mankind when he obeyed God and God ultimately saved Noah's family and destroyed the wicked. Abraham stepped out to follow God's direction even when he didn't understand it. Sarah, by faith, conceived in her old age and bore a son, Isaac, who became a child of promise and blessed Jacob and Esau. Jacob blessed the sons of Joseph, and Joseph predicted the departure of Israel from Egypt. Moses' parents were not afraid of Pharaoh and hid Moses for three months. Moses refused the label, son of Pharaoh's daughter, choosing instead to be known as the deliverer of God's people. Rahab received the spies in peace. On the stories go about many other of God's faithful throughout the Bible who had memorable moments in their lives affecting generations moving forward.

These accounts can be called "Donkey Jawbone Moments" for each of these men and women of faith. Donkey Jawbone Moments are times in the lives of these faithful when they rose to the occasion and took a stand of faith for which they are forever remembered. Even now, thousands of years later we still tell the stories of their heroic faith as well as the challenges in the midst of their faith. These Donkey Jawbone Moments have inspired us, warned us, guided us and prodded us along as we seek to discover our own measure of faith.

There are modern examples of faithful men and women who continue to leave jawbones of faith scattered about for us to find. You may be thinking of some right now.

I consider my grandfather, Basil Brownlee, to be a great man of faith. He came to know Christ at the age of 25 in an old-time Pentecostal church. He believed in the power of God and committed to prayer everything he did. My dad always claimed he married the daughter of a Texas oil man - literally translated, he owned a gas station.

Before pursuing a career in petro he owned a peanut farm. I remember many stories about how he prayed over his crops and on several occasions earned favor from the Lord. Stories told of times when it rained over his farm, yet not one rain cloud appeared over neighboring farms and these same neighboring crops were devoured by pests, yet never crossed over into his property. In my eyes, my grandfather was a saint. He inspired me to live a life dedicated to Christ and he passed forward many Donkey Jawbone Moments of faith, which continue to help me walk through difficult times.

There was a man from my home church whom after his death people still discussed his legacy. He was a man of the Word who spent hours memorizing scripture. I remember times in services when the Holy

Spirit came upon him and he walked to the front of the church and paced back and forth quoting by heart the Word of the Lord. His jawbone moments have prompted many to be students of the Word.

Who is the cloud of witnesses in your life...great men and women of faith who have left behind testimonies inspiring you to overcome great adversity? What are the stories you have stored in your heart and recall in your mind that keep you on the right path? We use these Donkey Jawbone Moments as weapons so we may claim victory against the enemies battling against us. The question becomes, what are the donkey jawbones we are leaving behind for future generations? What is the legacy for which we will be remembered?

A Legacy of Children

Some of the great witnesses mentioned in Hebrews were included because they raised and blessed their children. Sarah, long past the child-bearing age, was willing to bring a son into the world earning her a spot in the great hall of faith. Isaac, who had many attributes of greatness, was the second father in the list of patriarchs. Isaac showed great faith in his father by not resisting being placed on an altar of sacrifice when his father Abraham was being tested. Yet in spite of everything his name represented, he appears in the hall of faith because of his blessing of Jacob and Esau. Likewise, Jacob was listed for blessing his children.

One of the greatest testimonies of faith a parent can leave behind are children who continue living in the ways of the Lord. As Christian parents, we pour our heart and soul into our kids, "training up a child in the way he should go."[59] We constantly battle against the distractions of the world and snares of the enemy. Yet it is critical to win this battle.

My mom and dad were both raised in Christian homes and raised three preacher's kids. I'm fully aware of the reputation of preacher's kids. I choose to believe it is because they play with the deacon's kids. Seriously though, my siblings and I felt the pressures of living in a glass house as well as the expectations of others which often drive many P.K.'s astray. By God's grace and praying parents my brother, sister and I have continued to serve the Lord into our adult years. I have heard my mom ask the question, "What did we do right for all three of our kids to remain in the faith?" As a parent, it is easy to be hard on oneself and think you did everything wrong. I wish I had my parents' formula for parental success I could bottle and sell, but I'm not sure there is one. What I do know is they always lived a consistent life in front of us. They included us in their ministries and allowed us the freedom to own and internalize our own faith so we were not merely assuming their faith.

During the years my family traveled on the evangelistic field we carried literally everything we owned in the 4 X 8-foot trailer hitched to the rear of our Buick. One rainy day I sat in the back seat as we made our way to the next revival meeting. I was entertaining myself conducting a wrestling match between my left and right hands (this was before portable video games and back seat video players). Suddenly, an oncoming car lost control and swerved partially into our lane striking the front fender of our car. The impact caused the trailer to swing out into the path of the oncoming car. When the car plowed into our trailer, it sent everything we owned in a thousand different directions. I still have the vision in my mind of my mom's typewriter hanging from a tree by the ribbon, equipment and suitcases scattered all about, and my dad's Bible laying in the ditch with his sermons blowing in the wind. We chased down the sermons and he tucked them squarely into the pages of his Bible. He gathered us together, held his Bible up and said, "We still have God and each other. Everything is going to be okay." The jawbone moment my Godly father etched on my mind has been a powerful weapon I have used over the years that has helped me through some tough personal challenges.

Today, our two grown twenty-something children who also represent my parents' third generation, are serving God and carving their own paths of faith. Chanda, our daughter, who has long had a heart for missions, is thriving in her work serving as a secular college campus missionary. She leads a weekly discipleship group and helps other girls grow in their faith. Her missions work has already taken her to several countries in Africa and Central America. Chanda married a young man who shares her ministry heart. Jamin, our son, is also serving God in several areas of ministry. While in high school he turned his passion for skating into his mission hanging out with crowds most church people overlook. He started asking God to help him reach his friends. It took about a year-and-a-half, time and patience until finally one friend turned his life over to Christ. Jamin was so excited; he took on the responsibility of helping this new babe in Christ grow in his faith by first purchasing him a Bible and then attending Bible study with him each week. Week after week he drove his little white mustang to the skate park and loaded it full of kids to take with him to the youth service. It wasn't long before one friend after another came to receive Christ as their personal Savior. I had mixed feelings watching my son pull up to the church with six or seven people packed illegally into his tiny four-seater car, but how do you tell your son who is excited to bring friends to church he must turn some away? By the time Jamin graduated from high school his influence and outreach efforts had brought nearly 30 young lives to the throne of grace.

As a dad, what better legacy could I leave than seeing my two kids sold out to the purposes of Christ? Who knows what great things God has in store for their lives? I wish I could take all the credit for their successes, but there was a great legacy handed down to me by my parents, which my parents had received from their parents. The sacrifices my grandparents Ballard and Belle Alexis and Basil and Rachel Brownlee made in life to be men and women of faith have proved in time to be well worth their efforts. The donkey jawbones they left for their descendants are now being used to carry forward the torch of Christ to the fourth generation.

Sadly there are times when the children of precious men and women of faith choose to follow a different path. It breaks my heart when I see the children of friends turn away from their faith when their parents did everything they could to train them in the ways of Christ. These friends try desperately, even combing through their family history, to find answers explaining where they went wrong. Often they did nothing wrong.

God gives each person a free will. As badly as we may want for our children to follow the truth, sometimes the things of this world draw them in a different direction despite our best efforts. When this happens it is important to remain steadfast in prayer for the seeds sown to continue growing inside of them until one day they produce fruit in their lives.

Whenever any of our kids are coming for a visit and we know it will be late when they arrive, Terri and I make sure that the porch light is on so they will be able to see their way into the house. It is important to keep shining God's light so when the time comes, these wayward children will find their way back home.

Spiritual Kids

Frank Kennedy was an old-time evangelist who preached many a revival. One such revival was the church my grandparents attended, First Assembly of God in De Leon, Texas. This revival went on for a week and was, by all congregational measures, an utter failure. After a whole week of preaching only two little boys dressed in overalls and barefooted made their way to the altar. The evangelist left those meetings disappointed, thinking nothing had been accomplished. However, both of those little barefoot boys became ministers. One of the two, George Brazil, was a noted evangelist, pastor and eventually served as vice president of a Bible college, mentoring thousands of future pastors, evangelists and missionaries. Many have come to know the Lord as their personal savior because one man preached and two little barefoot boys found their way to the altar. What the church deemed as a failed revival became the Donkey Jawbone Moment for those two future ministers.

When you reach out and lead someone to Christ, they become your spiritual offspring, the fruit of your spiritual labor. If you have ever led someone to Christ, you know what a great moment it is in your life. You feel great excitement for them and fill with pride when they do great things for Christ. You desire to be there for them, mentoring them as they discover God's will for their lives. By "giving birth" to spiritual kids, you leave a legacy behind which makes a forever difference in their life.

As I mentioned earlier my dad grew up in a Christian home. However, he did not on his own make a commitment to Christ as a child. After graduating from high school in Harahan, Louisiana, a part of the New Orleans metro, he left home and joined the active Marines. Following basic training he served for a time in Okinawa, Japan. After returning from this service he was invited to attend a youth rally in Oceanside, California. With nothing better to do he accepted the invitation. The night of the rally he met a family who took an interest in reaching out to him. Although he did not immediately accept Christ, they continued to invite him to church and into their home where they showed him great love.

On one of his military leaves he attended a service at his sister's church in New Orleans. During the service, God reached him in a miraculous way and he gave his life to Christ. Upon returning to Oceanside, his adopted West Coast family was thrilled at his conversion and continued to mentor and love him. When he finished his time in the Marine Corps, he immediately enrolled in Bible school. Although my dad's ministry was always around Texas, Louisiana and the Midwest, this California family continued to stay in contact with him. I had the great blessing of meeting them. Their investment in the life of a young man living far from home became his donkey jawbone. My dad went on to minister to many others who came to know the Lord as their personal savior. Many victories have been won for the Kingdom of God because of this family's legacy of faith.

When you are teaching a Sunday school class, serving as a youth sponsor, taking in foster kids, ministering to unwed mothers or any number of things on an unending list of investments made in the lives of others, you are creating and leaving behind donkey jawbones. You may not think your influence matters, but it does. Your legacy of faith may just be the key responsible for changing someone's life.

My son was recently contacted by one of the kids he used to pack into his little Mustang on Wednesday nights. This kid just wanted to thank Jamin for taking him to church. Jamin may never know, on this side of heaven, the literal impact he made on kids' lives. Chanda may never see what becomes of the girls she mentors in her college discipleship group or the kids she played with while in Africa, but they will remember. As they look back on their lives someday it is the donkey jawbone moments when someone took the time to minister to them they in turn will pass on in ministering to others.

Great Accomplishments

Donkey jawbones also refer to great achievements in our lives which have made a positive impact for the Kingdom of God. This one may be a little more high profile than the first two. We see everywhere examples of organizations seeing a need and rising to the occasion by meeting these needs. Many times these organizations are started through much adversity and against all odds. I told you the story in an earlier chapter about Chaney and Jessica Phillips and their organization, B.I.G. Love Cancer Care. Their ministry will continue as a beacon of light to families long after the Phillips have claimed their rewards in Heaven. You no doubt know people in your town, maybe even friends of yours, who labor tirelessly doing a great work serving greater purposes than they ever intended.

A skinny, 27-year-old preacher named David Wilkerson from small town Pennsylvania saw an article in *Life Magazine* in 1958 about seven teenagers in New York City who were being tried for murder. He had an unexplainable heart of compassion for these teens and felt the Holy Spirit drawing him to New York. This story fascinated me as a youth as I read the account in his book, "The Cross and the Switchblade." This man had no business in the inner city trying to preach to gang members. His passion was beyond anything natural as he desperately fought for a way to reach out to this shunned segment of society.

He had major conflicts with vicious Mau-Mau's gang leader Nicky Cruz. One time Cruz asked David the question, why was he there and why was he trying to help him? David answered the notorious gang member with, "Because I love you." Nicky stood in the face of this fish-out-of-water evangelist and said, "I'll cut you into a thousand pieces." And again without hesitation David answered, "And every piece would still love you!" If you have not read the book "The Cross and the Switchblade," I suggest it as your next must read. The book is an amazing story of how one man followed the voice of God against the very gates of hell.

David Wilkerson went on to establish an evangelical addiction recovery program called Teen Challenge. This organization now operates more than 1,000 centers in close to 100 countries and has staggering success rates when compared to other competitive programs.

David Wilkerson was tragically taken in an automobile accident on April 27, 2011. I assume there are many who enter Teen Challenge programs around the world who may never hear the name David Wilkerson or know who he was. What they will find however, is a program that changed their lives by helping them break the addictions and find the saving grace of Jesus Christ. A young preacher from Pennsylvania accomplished great things by following the voice of God and his legacy is a massive donkey jawbone that today helps thousands find freedom from addictions and a relationship with Christ.

Great churches and denominations were built on the work and prayers of great men and women who we may never know by name. Yet their work continues long after they enter the gates of heaven. Every time someone walks the aisle of your church and prays the sinner's prayer, it is a tribute to the jawbones someone left behind.

William Carey was quoted as saying, "Expect great things from God; attempt great things for God." God has planted in each one of us a seed of greatness, a potential for making a lasting mark on this earth. Many waste their greatness on accomplishments which have no eternal value. Still others live their entire lives without even attempting one great thing. Whether they opted for the easy road, or were just afraid of failing, they squandered their God-given potential leaving no donkey jawbones of greatness behind for others.

If you have been waiting for the right opportunity to start doing great things, the time is now. Follow your calling. God has a legacy to build within you.

What Will You Leave Behind?

A friend of mine loves to quote this line from his mother, "Only a few people in the world are the movers and the shakers, the rest are just filler." This is completely false. There may be more visible and vocal people in the world who demand more attention and credit, but the truth is we all add value and contribute to the moving and shaking. Never undersell your importance in the Kingdom of God. Not only do you have the potential to influence others and accomplish great things through the way you live out your life, you will leave behind a legacy for generations to come.

I ask you this question again, who is in your cloud of witnesses? My grandfather left a legacy of love for the Lord, which continually drives me to serve Christ. My grandmother Alexis left a legacy which reminds me to remain positive even when the situation isn't ideal. My grandmother Brownlee's legacy is to always remember the "least of these." The first lead pastor,

Walter Helms, I served under as a youth pastor was a servant's servant. His legacy to me was seeing the importance in treating others as my brother. Howard Eudy's legacy will always be there to remind me of the importance of learning scripture and studying the Word of God. Although these life influences are no longer here on this earth, they have each left a mark on my life. Their donkey jawbones remain for me to use to achieve victory over the enemy every time he comes against me.

Voted Off the Island

John Donne is the author of the famous quote "No man is an island." Actually the full text reads as follows: "All mankind is of one author, and is one volume; when one man dies, one chapter is not torn out of the book, but translated into a better language; and every chapter must be so translated...As therefore the bell that rings to a sermon, calls not upon the preacher only, but upon the congregation to come: so this bell calls us all: but how much more me, who am brought so near the door by this sickness...No man is an island, entire of itself. ...any man's death diminishes me, because I am involved in mankind; and therefore never send to know for whom the bell tolls; it tolls for thee."[60]

We are not only intertwined in life, but have the potential to continue to be an influence beyond the grave. If you are trying to live as an island, I challenge you to vote yourself off of the Island and build something worthwhile to leave behind. It doesn't take money or fame to leave a legacy of greatness.

The Psalmist wrote, "...The righteous will be in everlasting remembrance."[61] If nothing else, leave a legacy of righteousness so when those who come after you face trying times, they can wield the jawbone of righteousness you left behind and be inspired to press on.

It is up to us to decide what kind of legacy we will leave behind. Life is truly just a vapor; may we not vanish without a trace. It is the jawbone moments you leave behind that will define your true legacy.

Chapter 8
Who's Riding Your Donkey?

The donkey featured in this chapter took a very special journey and in so doing made possible one of the greatest stories found in the Old Testament. "Then Moses took his wife and his sons and set them on a donkey, and he returned to the land of Egypt. And Moses took the rod of God in his hand."[62]

For 40 years Moses had lived in the land of Midian. One day he loaded his family on a donkey to travel a 400-mile journey from the land of Midian to that of Goshen in Egypt. The actual distance of the donkey's travel is a rough estimate because Midian was a large area and it is not known exactly where in Midian Moses was living at the time of his departure. The terrain they traveled over would have taken more than two weeks to complete by foot and donkey.

What was Moses' purpose for traveling to Egypt? Many answers come to mind. Perhaps, "he is obeying the voice of the Lord," or going "to deliver God's people out of Egypt." Both are correct, yet a more interesting question that comes to mind is: "Is this a new calling or was it Moses' purpose all along?" To find the answer to this question let's look a little closer at Moses' history. Was Moses supposed to even be in Midian?

Years ago some friends and I took a trip from Arkansas to Nashville, Tennessee. Our return trip home took an adventurous twist. We were nearing Memphis barreling full speed ahead on Interstate 40 at about one o'clock in the morning, eager to reach home, when all of a sudden there appeared out of nowhere right in the middle of the Interstate a traffic light. I've traveled enough to know this is not normal.

Apparently, we had missed an exit and our freeway had run out somewhere in the middle of Memphis. We proceeded through the intersection and pulled into an adjacent gas station where immediately a gentleman approached the driver's side window and met us with a hardy, "You lost?" I guess we must have had a lost look about us. I explained our misguided trek and he offered a round of directions to set us back on course. As we inched down the road he pointed us toward, it soon became clear we were in an unsafe area. We even joked among ourselves he probably called his buddies and said, "I got a car full of suckers coming your way!"

Luckily we soon stopped at a major intersection where I spotted a McDonald's a few blocks ahead and decided it was time to seek some more reliable directions. I pulled into the parking lot reassured by the sight of three police cars. However, my assurance sank to a new low when I walked up to the locked door and peered inside. The officers were questioning people and someone was mopping something off the floor. I then felt a greater since of urgency to get out of Memphis and fast. Eventually we found someone who got us back on track and we wasted no time crossing the Mississippi River into Arkansas.

Think back to when you were in high school. What were some of your ambitions and passions? Do you remember how you were going to conquer the world and accomplish amazing things? There are those few who are blessed at a young age to have heard the voice of God as he revealed His divine plan and purpose for their lives.

Take an inventory of where you are in your present life. Perhaps there was a time when you felt you knew exactly what God's plan was for your life but now as you look at where you are you realize you are miles from his plan. Sometimes life unfolds in ways we don't expect and we find ourselves in places we never anticipated. We knew at one time where we wanted to go, yet somehow we ended up "lost in Memphis." It sounds a little like a song title. I just wouldn't want it to be the song of my life.

Rise of a Slave

Moses was born into slavery. The new Pharaoh, who did not remember Joseph or where these Hebrews came from, felt threatened by their growing numbers and ordered every male child to be cast into the river. Moses' parents hid him for three months and finally built the famous basket in which to hide him by the river. The Bible tells us the basket was laid "in the reeds by the river's bank."

The basket was placed beside a river stretching more than 4,000 miles, yet it happened to be in the exact place where the Pharaoh's daughter bathed. God was definitely up to something incredible. Pharaoh's daughter found the baby and adopted the child as her own. By providence, God allowed Moses' biological mother to be his nursemaid helping to raise Moses.

At this point in the story what do you think was God's plan for Moses' life? We see in the stories of Esther and Joseph how God placed them in a palace to save his people. I believe this too was God's original plan for Moses. He was ordained to grow into a prominent place within the realm of Egypt so at the right time God would prompt him to lead his people out of bondage. Moses most likely felt this call on his life as scriptures tell of his sympathy regarding the plight of his fellow Hebrews. From his adopted position, he could have easily turned a deaf ear to their cries and lived a privileged life.

One day he took action to protect one of his brethren in distress and killed the oppressive taskmaster. Perhaps he thought he would be secretly heralded as a hero among his kin, much like a Robin Hood type of old, or an ancient Batman. He may have felt it was time to start his role in saving his people from their plight. Instead, he found his actions backfired. *Hero* wasn't the label he was assigned, but rather, *murderer*! He couldn't risk being tried and imprisoned on murder charges, so he fled the life he had known for his first 40 years.

Lost in Midian

Ironically, the Egyptian city of "Memphis" was most likely the capital of Egypt at this time, and Moses' home for his first 40 years. So technically, the time Moses was "Lost in Memphis" represents the 40 years he spent in Midian after leaving Memphis. The land of Midian was a vast desert waste land and instead of cities, the inhabitants lived as roving nomads. The Midianites, descendants of Abraham and his second wife, Keturah, whom he married after the death of Sarah, were mostly shepherds, camel herders and raiders, staying on the move as their provisions dictated. They lived as tribal people made up of many clans and families.

While looking for a place to hide in the desert, Moses stumbled upon a well where young ladies were trying to water their father's flock. A group of bully shepherds were harassing them, and Moses, still having a "save the day" attitude, jumped in and drove away the antagonists and helped the women draw their water. Next thing you know, Moses has a home, a wife and two kids. Isn't that a familiar story? One minute Moses is a prince in Egypt, the next he is in the desert with a family. It hit him so hard he even named one of his sons "I have been a stranger in a foreign land." Try putting that in those little blocks on an application.

Moses spent the next 40 years trying to forget his first 40. He abandoned the longing in his spirit to be the defender of his people. All of those feelings were behind him and he settled into his new life, lost in Midian.

If you have ever tried running from the call of God, you know you keep running right into God as He attempts to pull you back to what He has called you to do. Moses was on the back side of the desert doing what he had done for the last 40 years, tending his father-in-law's sheep. He is now 80 years old and doesn't even have his own flock of sheep.

Maybe he was trudging along thinking about what a failure his life had become when he had an undeniable encounter with God. Moses knew it was time to return to the call he had once felt. Somewhere deep inside him, though suppressed for many years, there was still a spark of passion waiting to be ignited. When God appeared to Moses, it lit more than a bush. The spark was fanned into a flame once again, and though reluctant, Moses set his sights toward Egypt and saving God's people.

When you have survived in Midian for a long time, comfort sets in, and you sometimes find it easier to stay where you are settled and secure than to move toward the unknown. It often takes a burning bush experience to awaken our hearts, restore our passions, and remind us of God's call in our lives.

Many sermons from this story have been preached centered around the following exchange: God said, "What is in your hand?" Moses replied, "A rod. And Moses took the rod of God in his hand."[62] This conversation between Moses and God yields itself to some powerful truths.

Let's not overlook what Moses did before taking the rod of God in his hand. "Then Moses took his wife and his sons and set them on a donkey, and he returned to the land of Egypt." He did not have this donkey when he fled his life in Egypt. This donkey was part of the life he had built for himself while lost in Midian.

When you pack to go on vacation you try to think of everything you may need. When you travel with children methods of entertainment become top priority. Before cars came fitted with entertainment systems and before video games were in the form of portable touch screens, parents had to get creative. On one such family vacation I precariously balanced an old-school television atop a milk crate between the middle seats of our minivan. I secured it with bungee cords to keep it all in place. With the game console plugged into a power converter my teenage son made use of his game console on our long road trip to Disney World. The back of our vehicle was loaded to the ceiling with suitcases and an ice chest full of drinks.

Moses didn't have such luxuries on his two-week journey to Egypt. It was not an easy trip. What he packed on his donkey was much more than his wife and children. As we take a closer look at this donkey we will see exactly what it was transporting.

The New You

"Then Moses took his wife…" Moses knew this wasn't just a temporary mission on which he was embarking. It was a life change. Naturally, he couldn't leave his wife behind. Moses and Zipporah were married soon after he arrived in Midian. They had been married somewhere in the neighborhood of 40 years. Zipporah represents the life Moses had built since he left Egypt. He was now a man of love, commitment and maturity.

When God gets your attention and calls you out of Midian and back to the purpose He had for you all along; He doesn't require that you be the same person you once were when He originally placed His call on your life. The refining and growth you have experienced in your life during your time in Midian are what will now give you the strength to pursue His purposes.

My wife and I like a lot of the same movies. We are suckers for a good sci-fi flick as we like adventurous stories with twisting plots. There are, though, a few differences on our list. I consider it pure torture to sit through the incessant mumblings of "Pride and Prejudice." She can watch it over and over again. A movie she considers utter persecution happens to be one of my favorites..."Tommy Boy!" Chris Farley is hilarious in his role as Tommy, a child who grew up in a life of privilege. His father built a successful company from the ground up. Everything was a game to Tommy and he never worked at anything. When his father died, suddenly his world changed as the company was in danger of collapsing. Rightful ownership of the estate belonged to Tommy but, and rightly so, no one had confidence in his ability to lead. Tommy and a company assistant, played by David Spade, took a road trip together in hopes of restoring confidence from their customer base, securing the sales crucial to saving the company and keeping the jobs of hundreds of employees from their small community.

Much was at stake, but at first Tommy was not at all up to the task. As the journey progresses Tommy finds his strengths and matures into the man who eventually saves the company. The movie ends with Tommy miraculously coming through and the employees, who had previously held little respect for him, rallying behind Tommy as they had his father before him.

Moses may have spent 40 years lost in Midian, but God put to good use the character he had developed on his journey. Perhaps originally there was a different path Moses was to take, a "plan A" so to speak. God is not afraid of the alternative routes we sometimes take, in fact, neither is He surprised by them. He can use these diversions along the way as stepping stones to help us mature and prepare for the time we will step back into His perfect will. God wasted no opportunity from Moses' detour to Midian. He used Moses' father-in-law to speak wisdom into his life when they made it out of Egypt.

We find great beauty in the scripture: "All things work together for good to those who love God to those who are the called according to His purpose."[63] When we are following the purpose of God for our lives, God can take all of those seemingly loose ends and tie them up into a dynamic package of purpose. We don't have to erase the things that have happened to us along the way or the mistakes we have made in order to start over, we only need to hear God's voice and move forward in His plan.

As Moses helped Zipporah onto the donkey for the trip back, his mind must have reflected on all he had become in his time in Midian. History shows the man he matured into, one of the mightiest leaders of all time. It was impossible for Moses to start over, but it was not too late for him to move forward.

Experienced Stranger

Zipporah had to scoot up over the shoulders of the donkey to make way for Moses' oldest son, Gershom. The name Gershom means "I have been a stranger in a foreign land." As Moses hoisted Gershom up onto the donkey he was reminded this place he now called home wasn't really where he belonged. Yet, while a stranger in this foreign land, he gained valuable experience which aided him greatly in the task ahead.

I spent two years gaining the technical training to be an industrial instrumentation technician. I had my diploma and a good transcript to show for it and I was ready for this highly-skilled field. I sent out 130 resumes all around the country, and five to Australia. I targeted companies looking to expand their technical workforce. The most common reply I received, if I received a reply at all was, "We are looking for someone with experience." This is a common experience among graduates entering the workforce today. Which brings up the question; "How can one get experience if no one will hire them?"

Experience is valuable, as there is often a wide gap between what you learn in a controlled environment and what you actually learn while in the field. Once I found a company willing to hire someone only with academic experience, I began to build the skills and knowledge necessary to move beyond an entry-level position as an instrumentation technician. Education is great but it cannot alone take the place of experience. Over time working in a specific position you learn how to anticipate problems, identify solutions and achieve positive outcomes without having to even think a lot about it.

If you have children, you have no doubt had conversations with them with the hope of keeping them from making the same mistakes you have made. Perhaps you have even shared the successes you have experienced along your way. As parents we do this because we have real life experiences which lend insight into life and a viewpoint our children don't have.

I live in a neighborhood where there is no single road leading directly to my house. For years, I have navigated over cell phones giving turn-by-turn directions to individuals trying to find my home. I usually stand out on my porch waving so visitors will know when they have arrived. I live on the corner of two intersecting roads, but they do not cross like a plus sign. The through street is offset by half a block, which really throws a lot of people for a loop. The pizza guy always gets lost and we have to flag him down, but for any friend I have instructed how to get to my home, I don't remember having to tell any of them a second time. Why do you suppose this is? Because they have already been to my house and from then on the path is familiar.

God would love to keep us from hardship and disappointment. It breaks His heart when we get lost in Midian and struggle to survive. Once He brings us through these times He has no intention of wasting our experience. There will be others who get lost and walk the same path we have walked, and we may be the only ones who can help them navigate the winding roads.

Moses spent 40 years watching a flock which did not belong to him. He led them to food and water. He protected them from wild animals. He kept a watchful eye for any thief who tried to separate a choice lamb from the fold. God watched over him as he developed quality shepherding skills, knowing there was another flock he would one day lead. While Moses spent hours alone watching sheep graze, I'm sure he occasionally thought about the life he once had, but quickly shook it off. Maybe he thought "this is my life now. There isn't anything else I am qualified to do. I'm too old to start my own flock. I'll just have to make the most of it." God still had a mission for him to fulfill, not a different one, the same purpose He had in store when He created Moses, and he wouldn't have to waste a single moment of his experience watching over someone else's sheep. God created and called Moses to watch over His chosen sheep.

The family from which Moses came was a priestly family. His father-in-law was the priest of Midian. You would think the Midianites, also descents of Father Abraham, would have worshipped Yahweh, the one true God. It is believed, though, through archeological findings, the people of Midian worshipped multiple gods...idols. There is evidence they may have worshipped gods such as Baal, Ashteroth and even the Egyptian god Hathor.

Moses was taught to worship the one true God by his biological mother, who served as his nurse maid. Somehow, with exposure to all of these other religious practices, Moses maintained a relationship with the God of his fathers. Even though his father-in-law may have worshipped false gods, one thing Moses learned from this family was...reverence.

We as Christians love the relational aspect of serving Jesus. We sing with enthusiasm "What a Friend we have in Jesus" and "I am a Friend of God." There is nothing wrong with any of these sentiments. When it comes to reverence and devotion, it seems some of the false religions of the world actually put us to shame.

The Muslim faith may be the root of a lot of unrest in the global society of today, but one thing you can say about them, they are faithful to their idea of god. They have rigid times throughout the day where they stop what they are doing to pray, and will go to great lengths to defend any slander against their prophet or holy book.

Many Christians will simply "try" to carve out five minutes to pray if they aren't too busy, and will shrink into the background if some loud mouth starts to bash Jesus or their faith. Another observation worth noting, there are far more religions other than Christianity knocking on my door to tell me what they believe than there are members of local Christian churches.

Moses was in a heathen environment. Yet, I believe he gained experience in how to reverence and respect God. He learned how to serve Him with abandon and to stand when the time came to step out. When you embark on your journey out of Midian and back to the call of God, don't leave Gershom behind. God will not waste one single moment of your experiences. This is part of His making "All things work together for good…"

Don't Forget Your Helping Hand

Moses turned to his second son, tucked his desert-weathered hands under his arms and hoisted him onto the donkey behind his brother. This son's name was Eliezer, which means "God of Help." Even though Moses had 80 years of growth and maturity, and a full repertoire of experience from which to draw, he still knew he would need the God of Help to accomplish this monumental task. It is evident from the burning bush narrative Moses was not a confident man. He had weaknesses he thought should disqualify him from the task. God convinced him he would not have to lead on his own strength and abilities. He would have an ever present help every step of the way.

Faith and fear are always at war. Any time you try to take a step in faith, there is going to be an element of fear battling to keep you from moving forward. Just when you think you work up enough faith to launch out, you retreat thinking, "I just don't think I can do it!" Well, of course you don't. God doesn't choose us for what we think we can do, He calls us based on what He knows He can do through us. We are simply the tool and He is the master craftsman.

It is amazing to watch a professional painter, mechanic or surgeon perform in their skill level. A comprehensive knowledge of their set of tools and how to use these instruments makes them successful in performing complicated tasks. I can just imagine a doctor calling out, "Scalpel," and the scalpel whines, "I don't think I'm the right instrument for this procedure. Maybe you should try the scissors or the bone saw." The tool arguing with the surgeon would be crazy because the doctor knows the tool he needs and calls for a specific tool when its purpose is required. The surgeon doesn't expect the scalpel to jump up onto the patient and make a precise incision; rather the surgeon takes the scalpel in his hand and performs the critical procedure in concert with the chosen instrument.

I know you are way ahead of me in this analogy. God doesn't require you to do anything on your own. He only wants you to be the willing tool He can direct with His talented and capable hands. I promise, The God of Help will be there with you every step of the way and you will find you can do more than you ever dreamed possible.

My daughter has taken multiple mission trips to Mexico as well as to several countries in Africa. The trips to Africa were for a month or more at a time. These were not journeys to cushy city outreach initiatives, but rather locations which required up to 24-four hour bus rides from the nearest city. What makes this applicable is the fact that Chanda is an extreme germaphob. She doesn't like to get dirty, and the eight-second rule for dropping something on the floor does not apply. If it touches the floor it is out. She brings sleeping bags to hotel rooms so she can sleep without touching the public linens and I should buy stock in hand-sanitizer companies. Her mother and I watch in amazement as we see the pictures of this neat freak lying on the ground and eating things of which we shall not speak. Then, there was the famous chicken incident.

In one area where they went to minister the team was split, staying in different host homes. As a gesture of good will it was suggested they bring a live chicken to offer to the host as a way of saying thank you. Each team member was given a living, dusty chicken and the birds were not too happy about it. Chanda rode on the back of a bicycle taxi, holding on with one hand and grasping a hen by the feet in the other. It was flapping and cackling all the way. Once in the home, she presented the chicken to the host. A short time later Chanda was given a dull knife hardly sharp enough to cut a stick of butter much less sever a chicken's head. Chanda has never been involved in taking the life of anything more than a bug and has certainly never skinned a critter. She stood on the hen's wings and secured the head while sawing back and forth with the knife. Eventually, the bird succumbed to its fate and the pot was readied.

Terri and I asked ourselves, "Is this our little girl...the same girl who will not even drink after another family member?" How could she do something that in normal situations was so out of character? It is because when she got on the plane she had with her the God of Help who wrapped His masterful hand around her and used her abilities in a skillful way. If she had been asked a month before, "Would you be willing to kill a chicken in a village in the Deep South of

Africa for the cause of Christ?" She may have replied, "I don't think I can." The path God leads us down will often take surprising twists and turns, but you will never have to walk it alone, for the God of Help is always and forever present.

God's Purpose is God's Purpose

God has a ministry, a passion and a purpose designed for each of us. At some point in your life you felt His flame. There was a pull you couldn't explain, but somehow you knew it was what you were created to do. A few manage to stay on their inspired path and pursue the passion God placed in their heart from a very young age. Most get lost in Midian, feeling derailed and lost. Some have built a new life far removed from their original call and the burning desires they once knew have almost faded. Often, in times of remembrance we wonder, "It is too late for me to do it now."

Sometimes it is the failures and the sins of the past which drove us to Midian. It may have just been life itself taking over and pulling you there unexpectedly. Maybe one decision made the difference between following your God-given dream and landing in the back side of the desert. The good news is God has not abandoned His purpose for your life. His purpose is still His purpose. It doesn't even matter how long you have been lost in Midian. Moses had been in Midian for 40 years and then at 80 God gave him a pathway back.

Recently my wife and I started walking for our health. Walking turned to some light running. Soon we had some church friends talk us into running in local 5k races. I ran in a 5k race which also had a simultaneous

10k run. I finished my race and sometime later the 10k runners started filtering across the finish line. Long after the second-to-last finisher crossed the line, Mr. Cecil came around the last turn. Mr. Cecil is 80 years old...and walks with a cane! Yet he ran the 10k track. I was quite ashamed of my 5k performance when an 80-year-old man with a cane completed twice the distance. I don't know Mr. Cecil or anything about his story. He may have been a runner all of his life, or maybe he started some time late in life to strengthen his heart. Either way, he would be well within his rights to say, "I can't run! My time has passed. I walk with a cane." Mr. Cecil is an inspiration to all the runners in the race because he doesn't let any of the obvious deterrents keep him from running his race.

You have a race to run. Maybe you have taken a detour and have been wandering for years, spinning your wheels and hoping for another shot. Well, God is ready for you to take your shot. It may take a burning bush experience or a direct confrontation with God for you to realize what you are meant to do. When you do get the message, pack up your donkey and head back to the will of God as fast as you can get there. The road back might be inconvenient, long and uncertain, but I promise you it will be well worth it. So, what are you waiting for? Giddy up!

Chapter 9
Donkey Intervention

The two most famous donkeys in the Bible would have to be the one Jesus rode when he made his triumphal entry into Jerusalem and the talking donkey of Balaam. Who would not love a story about a talking donkey?

My grandfather once had a parakeet named Johnny whose favorite thing to say was, "Johnny is a pretty boy." It was fun to try to get him to repeat phrases. You may have seen video clips of dogs and cats screeching out, "I love you," or something similar. While these occurrences of non-human vocalizations are entertaining, in no way do they compare with a donkey able to carry on a conversation with its master. Before we move on to the meat of the story, let me set up the scene just a bit.

The Children of Israel had escaped from Egypt and moved across the desert. Everyone in the region had heard of this 1 million-plus mob that seemed unstoppable. Moses led the people into the land of Moab across from Jericho. The King of Moab named Balak, feared them as they had recently defeated the Amorites and seized control of their land.

It may be noteworthy to mention Moab is a descendant of Lot. After Lot fled Sodom, his daughters caused him to get drunk and sleep with them. The child conceived between Lot and his youngest daughter is the father of the Ammonites; the child conceived between Lot and his oldest daughter is the father of the Moabites. Therefore, these nations are brothers to some extent. They really had nothing to fear from their brother nation at this time because God told Moses not to touch their land because it was the inheritance He gave to Lot. Balak was unaware of this promise and thought he was next on the conquer list.

He sent for a prophet named Balaam because he knew whomever Balaam blessed was blessed and whomever he cursed was cursed. He needed something to give him an edge and help defend him against this menacing nation who, as he put it, "licks up the land."

Balaam of The River

Other than being known as the son of Beor, Balaam's lineage is unknown. Balaam and Beor are two of the seven gentile prophets mentioned in the Talmud. The other five were Job and his four friends. Balaam was carrying on the family business and living in the area where he had grown up. In Numbers 22 it says Balaam lived by the river in his native land Pethor. There has been much debate with regard to the exact location. Many readings assume "the river" refers to the Great Euphrates River. Some translations of the Bible have chosen to interject "Euphrates" in place of "river" based on this assumption.

Assuming the location was the Euphrates, right above Syria, it was about 400 miles from Moab. This translates into a 20-day journey one way. The fact Balaam lived such a great distance away would explain why he had not heard of this large company of people who wandered out of Egypt when everyone else in the region had tracked their migration.

In 1967 an inscription was found on the wall of an excavated structure in Deir Alla, in modern Jordan. It is known today as the "Balaam Inscription." The inscribed prophesy begins with the words "Warnings from the Book of Balaam the son of Beor" and speaks of impending doom. Some findings in this area lend evidence suggesting Balaam was from this area and not from Northern Syria. This is also in agreement with some writings found in the Samaritan Pentateuch and Vulgate (late fourth century Latin translation of the Bible) where it declares Balaam lived in the land of Ammon, adjacent to Moab. This would have made it more likely for Balak to have known Balaam. It would also fit better with the narrative of Balaam's death by sword which occurred when the Israelites went to war against the Midianites.[64] If this in fact is the location, "the river" would have more likely been the Jabbok or Jordan River, not the Euphrates. Even though we don't know for sure which of these locations is accurate, it is fun to toss it around for the sake of discussion.

Prophet or Profiteer?

Balaam was known as a "seer," as most prophets were thought to be, especially by those who didn't understand the true God. It is obvious Balaam, although he was undoubtedly a prophet who spoke to and heard from God, also profited from his status. The question still remains, who was Balaam and what was his position with God? A quick search will turn up a wide variety of opinions on the matter, all with diverse levels of validity. A theory exists that Balaam was a powerful sorcerer who knew of God. Though he communicated with God he also performed the dark arts. Personally, I do not buy into this theory because he seemed to have too much respect for God. We see recorded multiple times where Balaam said he only spoke or did what the Lord told him. A man with this level of reverence for God doesn't appear to be someone who was a witch or sorcerer. Some say he was a false prophet. This would not be entirely true because his prophesies were fulfilled. Since everyone is entitled to a theory, here is what I believe ties together the scriptures about Balaam. Balaam grew up in the home of a prophet and was taught the ways of the Lord. There are many individuals outside of the lineage of Abraham who feared and served God. Balaam had the gift of prophecy and when he prophesied his prophecies were fulfilled.

As his reputation spread people sought him out offering money for him to prophesy over their lives. At some point Balaam strayed from his call as a prophet of God and dabbled with magic.[65] He turned a sacred gift into a money-making profession and sold his services to the highest bidder.[66]

Why didn't God take the gift of prophesy away and refuse to appear to Balaam again? Paul declares in Romans 11:29 the "gifts and the calling of God are irrevocable." We have seen examples in our current times where "fallen pastors" who committed sin against God continued to preach and souls were saved and healed under their ministries. Jesus says on the Day of Judgment many will say, "Lord, we performed miracles and cast out demons in Your name." Yet they will not be allowed to enter into Heaven.[67] Narratives like these offer further proof that God's message and His miracles are His own. How God chooses to deliver

His message to us is often surprising and this is where we pick up on our donkey story.

Making God Mad

Balak knew of Balaam's flawless reputation and with this looming threat there was no room for failure. A group of men were sent with the "diviner's fee" to hire Balaam to curse Israel. The messengers explained the situation and Balaam gave them lodging for the night while he inquired of the Lord. God came to Balaam during the night and told him not to go because the nation he was being asked to curse was blessed of God. Balaam sent the men away explaining he could not go with them because he had not received permission from the Lord to go. Good for Balaam. He sought the Lord and obeyed.

Balak wasn't pleased and sent men more noble and numerous than the first entourage who gave Balaam a blank check to perform the curse. Balaam stood firm at first, but the dollar signs were cha-chinging in his eyes. Again he told them to stay the night and he would inquire of the Lord. The next three verses can be a little confusing if we don't understand the actual narrative was much longer than these three verses capture.

On the surface it looks like God gave permission for him to go. Balaam goes and God is angry with him for going. Several things are at play here. We know Balaam has dual loyalties to both God and money. Matthew 6:24 teaches this wasn't something with which God was pleased. God had already revealed His will to Balaam yet he came back begging for allowance to go. I believe God relented to see if Balaam would come to his senses and stay true to what he knew God had told him to do. Balaam made the wrong choice, choosing to follow money rather than the will of the Lord.

I was the recipient of my very last spanking at 12 years old. I grew up in a loving home that believed in correction. Many today gasp at the thought of striking their child. Proverbs tells us foolishness is in the heart of a child and the rod of correction will drive it from him.[68] It worked pretty well on my siblings and I as all three of us stayed out of trouble and today are grown and still living for God.

It was a weekday and Halloween night. Some friends had invited me to go out into the neighborhood and throw water balloons. It was already starting to get late, but I begged and my dad gave in with a stern warning to be home by nine sharp. I scurried out with a bucket of liquid grenades. When I slinked back through the garage door at ten o'clock my dad was not amused. I had been warned. We took a trip out to the carport where he grasped my arm with one hand and wielded a belt in the other. As the leather said hello to my backside I repeated the phrase, "I won't do it again! I won't do it no more!" I meant it, too. Never again did I blatantly disobey my father. I had agreed to whatever my Dad required in order to get his permission and then I did what I wanted to do. I paid the price for it in the end...literally!

If you take the time to read some related scriptures (Deuteronomy 23:3–5; 2 Peter 2:15; Jude 1:11) you will find the true motivation of Balaam. He consulted God and talked of only obeying what God instructed. The problem was Balaam was a man of profit and looking for an angle to please his customers while giving the appearance of following God.

Saved by a Donkey

Balaam saddled his donkey and set out to meet Balak. Even though he gave lip service to God he could not hide his heart. God was not about to allow Balaam to curse His chosen people, so He sent an angel to wait along the path and slay Balaam. As they rounded a turn, our hero, the donkey, saw the angel and turned away into a field. Note: had Balaam been in tune with God, he would have seen the angel himself. Frustrated, Balaam hit the donkey and turned it back onto the path.

My grandfather Brownlee had a stubborn mule on his peanut farm. One day this mule refused to go into the pen. My grandpa tried pulling and pushing him, luring him with food and talking to him. Yet, the mule would not budge. Out of frustration my grandpa grabbed the ear of the mule and bit down on it with everything he had. When he let go, the mule dashed into the pen without any hesitation. Someone who witnessed the event asked, "Why did you bite the mule's ear?" My grandfather replied, "I had to get his attention." Mules and donkeys can be stubborn like that. Balaam thought his donkey had gone renegade so he naturally thought a thrashing would straighten it out.

Further down the path in a narrow passage the angel appeared ready with sword drawn. The alert animal dodged to the side crushing Balaam's foot against the wall. The totally clueless prophet lashed out and further beat this dumb animal in hopes of teaching it a lesson. The angel stood for a third time in a place with no room to avoid him. The donkey sat down under Balaam and wouldn't go another step. Balaam was livid and with the intent of forcing compliance offered a thorough assault.

Then, the miraculous part of this story occurred, the donkey spoke. He said, "What have I done to deserve all this beating?" I don't know about you, but if it were me and my donkey was talking I would respond, "Whoa! My donkey is talking!" Balaam didn't even give it a thought, he began talking back responding, "Because you have abused me! If I had a sword I would kill you!" he added. The donkey went on to plead his case asking Balaam if he had ever mistreated him as long as they had been together. Balaam said he had not. Suddenly, his eyes were opened and he saw the angel with sword drawn. The angel explained had the donkey not intervened he would surely have died by his sword.

A Donkey's Perspective

The donkey saw danger when Balaam could not and he took action to save them both. We have all been there. A friend about to make a terrible mistake does not even see it coming. You are standing on the outside with a front row seat to the looming disaster when the battle begins. You ask yourself, "Do I interfere? Is it my business? How do I handle this and maintain my friendship?" It is always complicated when we feel the need to intervene and keep someone from experiencing impending doom.

Years ago I found myself in a difficult situation with a good friend of mine. He made a quick decision to do something in his life about which frankly I had serious reservations. Several red flags were raised and I was worried about the decision he was making. Out of concern, I tried talking to him about it, explaining how I felt. As you can imagine, it didn't go very well. He only saw what he wanted to see and I was upset he wasn't willing to heed my warnings. Out of protest, I broke a promise I had made to him causing division between us for a period of time. I regret my act of betrayal to this day. Later we did patch things up and today he remains a close friend of mine. Unfortunately, his decision led to some hardship and heartache I wish I could have helped him avoid. I still wonder to this day if I should have gone so far with my attempt to intervene in the decisions he was making or should I have minded my own business and stayed loyal to my friend and his wishes?

We can easily find scriptures to support staying out of it, like "We urge you, brethren, that you increase more and more; that you also aspire to lead a quiet life, to mind your own business, and to work with your own hands, as we commanded you"[69] In 1 Peter we read, "But let none of you suffer as a murderer, a thief, an evildoer, or as a busybody in other people's matters."[70] Really, the words "busybody" and "murderer" appearing in the same sentence?

God opened the eyes...and mouth...of Balaam's donkey, because He did not really want to destroy Balaam. Reading this we find obviously there are times when intervention is acceptable and does not come under the definition of "busybody." Are there times when God opens our eyes to someone's peril to keep them from being destroyed? How do we know when it is safe to step in and when to mind our own business? One of the oldest questions in life is, "Am I my brother's keeper?"

Mandate to Intervene

There is a time to intervene, according to scripture. James writes, "Brethren, if anyone among you wanders from the truth, and someone turns him back, let him know that he who turns a sinner from the error of his way will save a soul from death and cover a multitude of sins."[71] When a fellow believer falls into temptation and their spiritual soul is in jeopardy, intervention is encouraged.

The story of Michael Oher is an inspirational tale of a young man taken in by a Christian family, who eventually became a notable offensive lineman for the NFL team the Baltimore Ravens. The story unfolded in the film "The Blind Side" which proved to be a huge cinema success. The phrase "blind side" describes the responsibility of the position Michael plays. The left tackle is tasked with protecting the quarterback from defenders who run in from an angle the QB normally can't see. If a quarterback is right handed, he instinctively turns his body to the right sideline with his back to the left side.

A defensive player will sweep in on the "blind side" and in a matter of seconds take the quarterback to the ground. The left tackle's main responsibility is to make sure the sneak attack from the QB's blind side does not happen.

Even the strongest of Christians has weaknesses, and the devil would like nothing more than to slide in on this blind side and cause us to stumble and fall. When we learn to be team players instead of solo acts we are better equipped to protect each other's blind side. When the enemy slips in unexpectedly with a tackling grip on a brother or sister, we must be there to help them stay upright rather than aid in the tackle.

Galatians 6:1-2 says, "Brethren, even if a man is caught in any trespass, you who are spiritual, restore such a one in a spirit of gentleness; each one looking to yourself, lest you too be tempted. Bear one another's burdens, and thus fulfill the law of Christ."[72] The key operator in this passage is "in a spirit of gentleness." It is seldom received well when someone is told they are making mistakes. Everyone wants to believe whatever they do is right. When you are the one who must tell them they are going astray it usually creates some tense moments.

The donkey tried several tactics to save Balaam. The first attempt was simply a redirection into the field and away from danger. James 1:14 says we are tempted by being led away by our own desires. The devil would never succeed in making you sin if he only tempted you with things you have no natural desire to pursue. For example, I have never had a drink of an alcoholic beverage. I can't even stand the smell of it. Not beer, whiskey or even wine. Even through my teen years it was never a temptation of mine. Any time I have been around it the experience has been very unpleasant.

One time I asked a friend how one can drink something that smells so awful. He replied it is an acquired taste. I've always had a problem with things said to be an "acquired taste." If you do not like something, then why force yourself to tolerate it until you can get used to it? My son feels the same way about green beans.

I do, however, like Mt. Dew. I have been drinking Mt. Dew since before I was born. Think about it for a minute if you don't get it. I remember getting icy cold

Dew out of the machine at the gas station my grandfather owned. I would sit in a chair sipping it down with the old fellows while listening to their tales. My friends all know this is my drink of choice. Anytime my church knows I will be attending a meeting someone makes sure there is at least one on hand.

I am also not a coffee drinker. It too is an acquired taste I'm told. Once, at a men's retreat, we were all standing around waiting for breakfast to be served and almost everyone was drinking their morning cup of Joe. My pastor walked in, sized up the situation and left driving the church bus down the street to a nearby convenience store. He returned in a few minutes with a Mt. Dew just for me. What a real friend and pastor he is! My love for Mt. Dew isn't an addiction, I just like the taste, and you have to drink something to survive. It is my survival kit in a bottle with ingredients including water, concentrated orange juice, brominated vegetable oil (yum) and an essential dose of caffeine.

However, if I found out one day it is a sin to drink Mt. Dew I would stop drinking them and switch to something like maybe lemonade. I'm sure, though, every time I saw a commercial or a display in a store I would feel the carbonated citrus sensation going down the back of my throat. As a matter of fact, I'm feeling a desire for one right now. If my friend saw me opening the cooler at the convenience store and reaching for the green bottle, he could spring into action and say, "Hey, Keith, I grabbed you a lemon-lime sports drink, my treat!" His quick action might be enough to make me snap out of it and follow my friend away from oncoming destruction.

Although my example may be a bit lighthearted, redirection could serve as a mild level of intervention.

It takes knowing our friends and their struggles in order to help direct them away from the "snare of the fowler."[73] Some desires have a much stronger pull and a simple redirection isn't enough to deter a slide down the road of temptation.

The second time the donkey intervened he crushed Balaam's foot against a wall and caused him pain. Balaam became so angry he lashed out and beat the donkey for his actions. I'm not suggesting punching your friend in the nose to get him to listen, which would not yield positive results. But sometimes this level of intervention requires hitting them with the blunt truth and calling out your concerns directly. Be prepared as you will likely be met with opposition and hurtful words. Before advancing to this level of intervention, make sure you are operating from a place of love and under the direction of the Holy Spirit and not for any self-serving motivation. I am in no way endorsing personal crusades in the name of personal convictions. Keep in mind this donkey saw an angel of the Lord with sword drawn about to kill his friend.

Before confronting your friend, pray for the wisdom and guidance of the Holy Spirit. Gather all the facts of the situation and make sure you are not making any undo judgments because you don't have the whole story. Prepare scripture to address the sin directly. It may be wise to consult your pastor for guidance. When you have fully prepared, meet with your friend and present them with facts and why you feel the path they are on is destructive. Share the scriptures with them relevant to the issues. Allow them time to explain their circumstances and feelings. Offer to pray with them and be their support. Assure them you are on their side and do not want to see them hurt. Ask if they will allow you to partner with them for accountability. If you have gone to this length to prepare yourself for this level of intervention, you should be willing to do whatever they will allow you to do to help steer them away from sin and toward a better direction.

There is always the possibility they will resent your efforts, as Balaam did, and lash out at you, saying hurtful things. It won't be productive to retaliate equally at this point. It may take some time for your efforts to bring about results. It may also mean level two is not going to be enough to deter them from their path.

In Balaam's case, he abused the donkey for his efforts and continued in his fateful journey. This was indeed an extreme case. Sin often has a blinding effect, keeping us from seeing clearly the danger ahead. The goal of any level of intervention is for the other person to recognize the danger they are facing. When Balaam saw the angel for himself he became repentant.

The third time the donkey attempted to sway Balaam, he pulled out all the stops and just sat down, making it impossible for Balaam to continue. This scenario is too complex to be covered in this writing. It may require involving a pastor or others closely tied to a threatening situation to lovingly intervene. This is the step best described as "whatever it takes."

Jesus said, "What do you think? If a man has a hundred sheep and one of them goes astray, does he not leave the ninety-nine and go to the mountains to seek the one that is straying?"[74] Much too often when someone falls into sin the church body around them simply shrugs it off with a "That's too bad" attitude and moves on. We are encouraged to bring them back from their wandering state and restore them into the fold.

Ezekiel speaks boldly to this scenario saying "So you, son of man: I have made you a watchman for the house of Israel; therefore you shall hear a word from My mouth and warn them for Me. When I say to the wicked, 'O wicked man, you shall surely die!' and you do not speak to warn the wicked from his way, that wicked man shall die in his iniquity; but his blood I will require at your hand. Nevertheless if you warn the wicked to turn from his way, and he does not turn from his way, he shall die in his iniquity; but you have delivered your soul."[75]

Not Sin Related?

What if the issue at hand is not related to sin, but rather a friend or family member, maybe even a grown child in the throes of making a huge mistake? Scripture does not give us a charge to intervene for reasons other than sin. There are, however, some guidelines with regard to our relationships with one another in Christ.

1 Corinthians 12 has a lot to say about how interconnected we are as the body of Christ, saying whatever harms one part of the body affects the entire body. You wouldn't have to look very hard to find verses on comforting one another, edifying, having compassion for and loving each other. A few great references to keep forefront in your mind are: Colossians 3:16; 1 Thessalonians 5:11; Hebrews 3:13; 1 Peter 3:8 and 1 John 4:7.

It is okay to discuss with someone, out of love and concern, their decisions and offer to pray with them about their choice offering perspective based on your experiences. When it comes down to it, we are all responsible for finding the road God has laid out for us individually. It is a bold move to suppose you know God's will for someone else's life. If a loved one does make a bad choice, be present and available to help them up and love them. There is no love reflected through the words, "I told you so."

Balaam's End

Though the donkey tried to keep Balaam on the straight and narrow road, he fell into allegiance with Balak and the people of Moab as well as the Midianites. He refused to curse outright God's people, yet he advised Balak on how he could cause Israel to fall out of God's protection by persuading them toward idol worship and sexual immorality. After what became known as the "Peor Incident" (Numbers 25; 31:16), Israel fell into such wickedness the Lord struck them with a plague ultimately taking the lives of 24,000. In retaliation, as one of his last acts as leader of the House of Jacob, God gave Moses an order for revenge. Moses took 1,000 from each tribe, 12,000 in all, and attacked the Midianites resulting in great slaughter. Among the dead was Balaam, son of Beor. We met Balaam at the beginning of this story trying to resist being hired by Balak yet he ended up living among and dying with the people of Midian. The Sanhedrin text recorded Balaam as around 34 years of age when he died. With his ability to communicate with God and hear the voice of the Almighty, he could have been a true prophet, but was turned aside due to his own greed.

Sometimes despite our best efforts to intervene, as illustrated by the donkey in this story, the ones we care about may still choose to follow a destructive path. The risk of having our efforts rejected should never discourage us from trying to be a watchman doing everything we can to steer our brothers and sisters away from the angel of death in the path.

Chapter 10
A Donkey's Redemption

The Holy Bible is filled with the mysteries of God, some of which He graciously reveals to us through the Holy Spirit. Still others remain difficult for our human finite minds to fully comprehend. The sermons and teachings of some of our greatest theologians dance around these subjects with grand words and analogies, yet fall short in lending complete understanding. The subject of this chapter's donkey tale is just one of these enigmas.

Let's start with a text we find in Exodus 13:11–13 and again in 34:19–20, "And it shall be, when the Lord brings you into the land of the Canaanites, as He swore to you and your fathers, and gives it to you, that you shall set apart to the Lord all that open the womb, that is, every firstborn that comes from an animal which you have; the males shall be the Lord's. But every firstborn of a donkey you shall redeem with a lamb; and if you will not redeem it, then you shall break its neck..." Why do you think the donkey is singled out in such a way? Why can't a donkey be offered to the Lord? These questions deserve exploration for sure.

The question I believe we will never fully understand on this side of heaven is *why does God require a blood sacrifice to cover sin*. There is no shortage of long dissertations on this subject, though I equate them to man trying to explain supernatural laws in human terms. We may not be able to comprehend the *why*, but it is established as fact by scripture.

Terri and I home schooled our two children through eighth grade. In many ways this was a blessing yet in other ways it felt more like a curse. Our daughter's learning style is to understand all the theory behind the facts before she will accept it as truth. The desire to thoroughly understand something before one believes it is a positive attribute - except when it comes to math formulas. In math it is much more useful to just accept the rule and move on. During one particular teaching session I was trying to explain how to work a page full of problems using familiar formulas. Chanda didn't want to use the formula unless I proved to her where the formula came from and why it should be trusted. I finally told her men and women had devoted their entire lives to figuring out one formula and shared it for free so the public could work the problems without having to devote their entire lives trying to figure out how the formula works. Some things we just have to accept as proven rules of life and use them the way they were intended in order to make progress.

I apply the same philosophy to God's laws. I believe we should study intent on understanding all that we can. Then by faith we need to accept what we aren't able to fully grasp. Whether I fully understand the *why* doesn't make the law any more or less a fact. When it comes to the covering of sin we do have ample scripture to guide us through what we need to know.

Fatal Sentence

First, we all know the mandatory penalty for sin is death.[76] God is completely holy and righteous and nothing unholy or flawed can access His presence. When His creation breaks His sacred law, death is the sentence. Our fate would be sealed if it were not for a merciful God who allows payment to be made by proxy, as long as the penalty for the sin is served. This proxy payment must still be in blood. Hebrews 9:22 reads, "...without the shedding of blood, there is no forgiveness." After the original sin against God was committed by Adam and Eve sin was ushered into the world. God set the precedent by slaying animals to cover the nakedness of Adam and Eve.[77]

One Wednesday night after our young adult church service I took a small collection of leaders to a local Mexican restaurant to discuss strategy and ideas for advancing the ministry. There were only two other tables in the dining hall that were occupied so the place was fairly vacant. A gentleman dining alone was at one table and sitting just a few yards away was a family from our church. We had been there only long enough to receive our drinks when we heard a loud booming voice coming from the entrance and yelling, "Help! Somebody help!" I immediately looked over to see a tall, large-framed man standing in the doorway completely naked. He continued calling for help. I instantly told the group at my table, especially the young ladies not to look. I wondered when a manager would respond to the situation. No one seemed to want to approach the man who was obviously in a mind altered state. The bare man walked further into the room and was now saying, "Get 'em off me! Get 'em off me!" A manager finally emerged and asked, "Get what off of you?" The man replied, "Snakes! They are all over me!" All of a sudden he spotted two bus boys who had come out of the kitchen and took off running toward them. The frightened young men retreated back to the kitchen with the naked man in hot pursuit. They circled back out of the other kitchen door followed by their unrelenting pursuer. When the man exited the kitchen the manager stood holding a tablecloth suggesting he put it on. The man would have nothing of it, "There are snakes in it!"

My group was praying for all they were worth and I was hovering like a mother hen feeling responsible for bringing them into this situation. The unclothed man approached our table and I asked him to move along. I honestly was at a total loss as to how to handle this situation as was everyone else in the room. He moved past our table when the lady from our church seated at the other table attempted to calm him down and take the table cloth. Eventually, the police arrived, covered him, and escorted him out. The man was in bad need of a covering! God's care for the first couple served more than a physical covering for their nakedness. The covering of Adam's and Eve's nakedness is symbolic of Jesus' shed blood on the cross covering our sin.

Abel offered a more excellent sacrifice than Cain because it was a blood sacrifice of the firstborn of his livestock and was without blemish. Cain's offering of produce was an example of self-redemption, a picture of man trying to do it his own way.[78] When the Mosaic law was given, sacrifice was explained in detail, outlining the type of animal to be sacrificed and for which trespass. The text for this chapter explains these laws demanding every firstborn among the animals be given to the Lord as sacrifice, except for the donkey. The donkey was not worthy to be sacrificed therefore a lamb was required to be the sacrifice in its place allowing the young donkey to live. The owner had the power to choose either to sacrifice a lamb in its place and allow the donkey to live, or to administer the punishment to the donkey for being unworthy of sacrifice to the Lord.

Unclean and Unworthy

Why was the donkey unworthy of sacrifice? Because the donkey is on the list of unclean animals and unworthy of human consumption or sacrifice. All unclean animals would be subject to this law, but the donkey was the most common possession of an Israelite. The donkey was in a difficult position because the firstborn of all animals belonging to a family in Israel had to be completely given to God. Only clean animals without blemish could be sacrificed. Since the donkey was unclean, it did not qualify as the sacrifice requiring a proxy sacrifice be made in its place... a lamb worthy of sacrifice.

Throughout the book I have asked you to relate to each of the donkey's we have found buried in the scripture. More than any of the previous donkeys the donkey in this chapter exemplifies the position we are all in. The end of our text says, "And all the firstborn of man among your sons you shall redeem." We don't have to compare ourselves to this donkey; the scripture spells it out for us. In the same way that a donkey must be redeemed, so does the firstborn of man. When Adam sinned, it transferred the name of man to the unclean list and made us unqualified to be the sacrifice for our own sin.

I remember as an early teen I spent time with some other neighborhood boys playing a little street basketball. We divided into teams and played full press on an outdoor asphalt court at a local elementary school. I wasn't the greatest athlete and quickly dispensed of the ball as though it were a hot potato any time it would accidentally wander my direction. One day that all changed. The ball landed in my hands, I sized up the situation and saw that I had a clear path to the goal. I took a step and the basketball dribbled under my hand as time slipped by in slow motion. In my head I could hear the gym-like echo of the ball with each strike against the asphalt and the roar of the crowd. My teammates and defenders alike were left in my wake. Without an ounce of opposition I lifted the ball toward the goal for the layup and a couple of gentle bounces later it slipped gently through the net. My teammates were shocked, and the other team was rejoicing as I had just made a basket on their end of the court. Needless to say I wasn't ever picked first, especially after such a display of incompetence.

When Adam and Eve dribbled the ball down the wrong end of the court and scored for the opposite team it put a black mark on all of mankind. No longer would we be allowed to be picked first to play because we are all scarred by sin. Isaiah 64:6 says, "But we are all like an unclean thing, and all our righteousnesses are like filthy rags..." Even at our very best we are unworthy to be our own sacrifice for sin. We are unclean animals in need of redemption by a lamb. God had a choice to make. He could allow man to go without sacrifice and face the punishment of death, or because of His love for us He could send a spotless lamb to be sacrificed in our place so we might live.

A Pain in the Neck

The method in which an unredeemed donkey was to be executed was very specific. Out of hundreds of ways God could have ordered the death of a donkey without sacrifice, He demanded its neck be broken rather than it being stabbed, cut or bludgeoned. God did not leave the method up to the executioner by just saying, "Kill the beast!" He prescribed the exact method of termination. Let's ponder that a bit.

A donkey has a short, stout neck, well proportioned to its short, stocky body. It would not be an easy task to break such a strong neck. The sentence was carried out by striking the animal at the base of the neck with a blunt object. The method of the execution had to be as far from a true sacrifice as possible. All sacrificial land animals were prepared by severing the major blood vessels located at the neck, but never by breaking the vertebra and severing the spinal cord. The exact opposite would be done in the case of the donkey. The spine had to be broken at the neck without spilling blood so no confusion would be perceived suggesting a sacrifice.

Before we get too up in arms over bashing a donkey, we must understand the scripture is not advocating the killing of donkeys. These were prized and beloved animals held in the highest esteem. In the Ten Commandments, donkeys were among the few explicitly named creatures not to covet, along with wives, servants and houses. In Exodus chapter 21, if a donkey fell into someone's pit the donkey had to be compensated for. If a donkey was stolen, double payment was required of the thief.[79] The Sabbath was not only a day of rest for men and women, but Exodus 23 declares it a day of rest for the donkey as well. There was certainly no ill will toward them.

Want a Cookie?

The point of the scripture was redemption. Though a choice was proposed, who would choose to slaughter their new foal when a way of escape was outlined for them? I visited my sister in Arlington, Texas. I was watching a short-lived television episode of "Who Wants to be a Super Hero" hosted by the famous Stan Lee along with my five year old nephew Asa. He was munching on some sugar cookies when he pulled one out of the bag, waved it in front of my face, and said in his high-pitched, super-cute, little boy voice, "Uncle Keith, want a cookie?" I love cookies but have realized the older I get the less of them I need to consume lest I start having trouble tying my shoes. So I responded as kindly as possible, "No thanks, Asa. I don't really want one right now." He wrinkled his face in a bewildered gesture and squeaked out in a questioning tone, "It's a cookie." He couldn't believe someone would turn down a cookie. Did I not realize the goodness that he was waving in front of me? I must be missing something.

To think that someone would not redeem their new foal with a lamb was incomprehensible. Of course the donkey would be redeemed. In the same way, Jesus became the sacrificial lamb sent to redeem us from a sentence of death and give us a life of fulfillment and blessing. Yet so many look at this free gift of redemption and say, "No thanks. I don't want my life to be saved from death. I'll just continue down the path of destruction." I'm sure God feels a lot like Asa did with his cookie offering. "I'm offering you life for death," He must think. I do not believe God gets confused, but He would have every right to scratch His head in disbelief when mankind turns away from the greatest gift ever given as though it was of no real value.

God had a term for Israel's refusal to live for Him. Eight times he referred to Israel as a "stiff-necked people," and there are eight additional references to the nation stiffening their necks and not listening to the Word of the Lord. Stephen called the council of priests "stiff-necked" to their face and it made them so mad they immediately stoned him. We get a picture, now, of the similarity between the literal stiff neck of the donkey which must be broken if not redeemed and a stiff-necked people who face a broken death if they do not accept the redemption offered.

One day, while in the fifth grade at Ridgecrest Elementary School in Ridgecrest, Louisiana, I was in the classroom minding my own business when a fellow pre-adolescent surprised me by shoving a little hand scribbled note into my hand. I unfolded the trimmed down sheet of loose leaf paper and read the penciled message, "Will you go with me…" I could literally stop right there because you have already finished the sentence. If you are a more seasoned person you remember when these notes would circulate. I'm sure if the same ritual is practiced in modern times it is sent via text or social media. In case you don't know the rest of the note, it continued with, "Check yes or no."

Following was the signature of a young lady that will forever remain anonymous.

Now I had nothing against this girl. She was a cute little brunette with a short haircut and really friendly personality. However, I wasn't interested in having any girlfriend at all. After all, it was the fifth grade. I had more important things to do than have a girlfriend, like running through the woods shooting birds with my BB gun. Who needs a girl complicating their life, right? So I did the only right thing to do; I checked "no." This is where all the guys go, "Yeah!" and all the girls say, "Aw, that's so mean!"

I've always been the kind of guy that hates to be misunderstood, so to make sure there were no mixed signals being sent I took my number two pencil and wrote at the bottom of the page, "no no no no no no no no no no no no no no no no..." Before you cast judgment on me for being immeasurably cruel please know I did not intend to hurt the young lady's feelings. Quite the opposite. Isn't it the worst thing a guy can do to lead a girl on? My mother raised me to be a gentleman and so I did the only gentlemanly thing I knew to do so I could never be accused of leading a girl on, I turned the paper over and wrote, "no no no no no no no no no no no no no no no no no no no..." completely filling the back of the paper.

When we pick up the Word of God, we are literally holding in our hands a love note written by the creator of the universe who redeemed our sinful, unclean state with the spotless lamb of His Son, Jesus Christ. In John chapter 14 Jesus explains the only way to be redeemed to the Father is through himself. He promised upon leaving this earth his time would be spent preparing a place for us so we can forever be with him. We have his message in our hands saying, "Will you go with me, yes or no."

I'm confident you can remember the time in your life when you stood holding that note and checking yes to serve the Lord. Over the years you may have reaffirmed your commitment by penciling in extra yeses at the bottom of the paper and possibly even turning the page and filling the back with a repeated yes. We all, though, have family and friends, co-workers and neighbors who have either checked no, or they are living their lives trying to avoid the question altogether. The blunt reality is one day there will be a judgment and those who have not accepted the gift of redemption will have a penalty to pay. They held their necks stiff for too long and in the presence of Almighty God the stiff neck will be broken as they bow their knee and confess, but it will be too late.

Paul stated in his second letter to the Corinthians, "We then, as workers together with Him also plead with you not to receive the grace of God in vain. For He says: "In an acceptable time I have heard you, And in the day of salvation I have helped you." Behold, now is the accepted time; behold, now is the day of salvation."[80] Yet, very few feel this urgency. There is always tomorrow, or when I'm older. It is up to those of us who have experienced redemption to bring our stiff-necked donkey friends to the point of understanding before they must face the Day of Judgment.

Our Choice

The part of this analogy that differs when applied to our redemption is our own free will. When a firstborn foal made its appearance, the Hebrew owner made the choice to redeem it with a lamb and performed the sacrifice completing the redemption. In our case, the sacrifice was made, but we still have free will to accept or deny its application to our lives.

I can't imagine the donkey rebelling against the sacrifice and demanding his neck be broken. The devil didn't launch all the demons of hell to make sure the donkey accepted its own fate. Satan has indeed gone to great lengths to separate man from redemption and our overcoming his wiles to bring our fellow donkeys to Christ is often quite a challenge. It would be awesome if everyone you gave the plan of salvation to burst into tears and fell to their knees. More often the scenario is a longer process requiring the seeds planted by multiple sowers be cultivated before a place of repentance is reached.

My son and I acquired, for next to nothing, a 19-foot cuddy cabin cruiser. You get what you pay for, right? The boat was in very rough shape, though it had some promise. It had gone through several men's hands who intended to fix it up but never got around to it. The hull seemed in good shape and what you could see of the Mercury Mercruiser inboard/outboard motor seemed like it might even crank. We hailed it as a great father/son project. The first step we took was to clean out all the trash and debris to see with what we had to work. It was important to know if the motor would turn over before we sunk any more time and money into it, so we changed the plugs and oil and emptied into it a five-gallon can of gas. Being there was no ignition switch present I had to trace out and hot wire it. The motor fired right up, drawing shouts of elation from both of us. The project was on.

Over the next year and a half we spent many hours together on that boat. We had to remove all the old rotten flooring and replace it with new marine grade ply wood, lay fiberglass over the floor and replace old carpeting. We completely re-painted the boat from bow to stern, cut out and covered new side panels with vinyl and cord trim, and purchased new seats. A motor cover had to be designed and built and a new control panel installed and wired. The project was longer and more demanding than we originally envisioned and the whole time we worked on our boat we looked forward to the day we would cruise across the lake with the wind blowing through our hair. With some more tuning to the motor the day finally came to put it in the water. It was a very exciting day indeed, filled with the benefits from a long process, and very much worth it. We christened her the "Rachel Belle" named after my two grandmothers, Rachel Brownlee and Belle Alexis.

Helping our family and friends find redemption can be a lot like a boat renovation. They may look pretty rough to the casual observer, or may have been given up on by others who tried to reach them, yet when we look at them through the eyes of Christ we know there is potential for them to accept the price of redemption. With some time and patience and a lot of guidance we work toward one day seeing them sail down the river of life with a new name written in Glory.

In one strange sounding law we find the root of the greatest gift God has to offer us. He chose to redeem us with a lamb so we could have eternal life. I am so glad I accepted redemption for myself rather than be counted among the stiff-necked donkeys in this world.

The Donkey's Tail

During the Sunday school quarter I taught this series, donkeys seemed to be permanently identified with me. Friends and church members texted me photos of donkeys they saw or links to stories about donkeys. Once while my pastor was preaching, a donkey was mentioned in the text he was reading and he stopped and said, "Where's Keith?" I was thankful everyone took such interest in ten stories about a little gray, long-eared beast of burden that so easily went unnoticed. There is certainly plenty we can learn from them to strengthen our walk with Christ.

In the introduction I told you about the small concrete donkey my grandparents displayed in their street side rock garden and how it now resides at my parents' home in Louisiana. A few years ago they walked out of their house and discovered the donkey was stolen. When they informed my brother, sister and me, we were deeply saddened by this loss. Scores of childhood memories were wrapped up inside the monetarily valueless sculpture and we couldn't imagine who would steal such a thing. We were ready to converge upon the town and form a posse to canvas all the neighborhoods with pitchforks in hand. Soon we accepted our beloved yard ornament was lost forever. Sometime later, a friend of my parents called and asked, "Didn't you have a little donkey, which sat in your front yard? I think I saw it behind a house today." The police were called and with much celebration the donkey was returned to its rightful place. It turned out it was the act of some mischievous teenagers.

When you study God's Word, even if the subject of the study is a lowly donkey, we are responsible to hide those lessons in our heart and cherish them. Our adversary would love nothing more than to steal these truths away and keep them out of reach. Don't let the enemy steal your donkey! Protect the things God teaches you and pass them down to your children.

Eeyore was always losing his tail. Once after re-attaching, Christopher Robin asked if he put it on properly. Eeyore responded, "No matter. Most likely lose it again, anyway." We do not have to show this low level of confidence with the Word of God. We can truly hide His Words in our heart, even if those words are about a little donkey.

References

1. Genesis 1:24
2. Genesis 49:14
3. Genesis 30
4. Deuteronomy 33:18
5. 2 Chronicles 30:18–20
6. 2 Corinthians 5:17
7. Jeremiah 23:23–24
8. Mark 16:15
9. Romans 8:28
10. Isaiah 43:19
11. Luke 10:30–35
12. Galatians 6:2
13. Matthew 6:1–4
14. 1 Kings 13:8–9
15. 2 Timothy 1:7
16. Ephesians 6:13 (paraphrased from NKJV)
17. Colossians 3:13
18. Ephesians 4:14
19. Philippians 1:3–6
20. Galatians 6:9
21. Joshua 17:15; 19:50; 20:7
22. Joshua 17:18, Jeremiah 50:19
23. National Treasure (2004)
24. John 11:54
25. Hebrews 10:35–36
26. Acts 19
27. Psalm 37:7
28. Job 11:7
29. Job 11:12
30. Proverbs 3:5, 6
31. Mark 6:48
32. 1 Samuel 1:1
33. Psalm 37:23
34. Genesis 36:24
35. Genesis 36:15-19
36. Psalm 63:1
37. Genesis 26
38. John 7:37–38
39. Genesis in 26: 34
40. Numbers 13:1–3
41. I Samuel 25:3
42. Joshua 7:21
43. 2 Samuel 14:26
44. Judges 17:4
45. Luke, 22:19, 2 Corinthians 12:9
46. John 8:7
47. Galatians 5:22
48. Matthew 7:16
49. Hebrews 5:12–14
50. John 12:24–25
51. Matthew 21
52. Proverbs 15:1
53. Romans 12:18
54. Ephesians 4:26–27
55. I Samuel 25:24–31
56. Romans 12:17–21
57. Acts 18:18
58. Hebrews 12:1
59. Proverbs 22:6
60. *Devotions upon Emergent Occasions and Seuerall Steps in my Sickness - Meditation XVII,* 1624, John Donne
61. Psalms 112:6
62. Exodus 4:20
63. Romans 8:28
64. Numbers 31
65. Joshua 13:22
66. 2 Peter 2:15; Jude 1:11
67. Matthew 7:21-23
68. Proverbs 22:15
69. 1 Thessalonians 4:10–11
70. I Peter 4:15
71. James 5:19–20
72. Galatians 6:1–2
73. Psalm 91:3
74. Matthew 18:12
75. Ezekiel 33:7–9
76. Romans 6:23 (The Holy Bible, New Living Translation, copyright ©1996, 2004, 2007 by Tyndale House Foundation. Used by permission of Tyndale House Publishers, Inc., Carol Stream, Illinois 60188. All rights reserved.)
77. Genesis 3:21
78. Hebrews 11:4
79. Exodus 22:4
80. 2 Corinthians 6:1, 2
81. Psalm 139:1-10
82. Luke 6:39

Made in the USA
Charleston, SC
22 April 2014